"Children need fathers w̲̲̲̲̲̲ ̲̲̲̲̲̲ ̲̲̲̲̲̲ ̲̲̲̲̲̲ Jesus says, 'The Son can do nothing by himself. He does only what he sees the Father doing,' He is explaining that His life and work here on earth is a reflection of what God the Father is modeling. The supernatural masculinity Jesus reflected in the Gospels had its source and substance in the Father.

Jim Bradford believes, as I do, that God intentionally modeled masculinity *for* us to show it *through* us. Thank God for *Masculinity by Design*, which puts this information into practical and biblical context for men and their families, modeling the Father's heart as Jesus' heart. More than ever, we need Christlikeness modeled in the home, and the book you hold in your hand is your map to follow."

—Kenny Luck,
author of *Dangerous Good: The Coming Revolution of Men Who Care*, founder of Every Man Ministries

"This book is a must-read for all who truly want to be on God's championship team. Jim Bradford was known as Coach Bradford to one of my mentees, Ricky Sailor, when he was in high school. Ricky called me early one Sunday morning and invited me to his church to hear Coach Bradford preach. Jim's message was 'Many Options, but One Choice.' After my NFL-playing days ended three decades ago, I was presented with many options, but there was only one choice.

Jim's book will help you make the right choice when you come to a crossroad in life. Journey with someone who has traveled the journey. *Masculinity by Design* is a playbook that is going to produce winners in the Greatest Game of All . . . the Great Commission."

—Tyrone Keys,
retired NFL player with Buccaneers,
Chargers, and 1986 Super Bowl Champion Bears

"I've known Jim Bradford, aka Coach Bradford to me, since I was sixteen years old. Many of the teachings he is providing in his new book, *Masculinity by Design*, have been piercing my ears, heart, and soul for twenty-five years. His perspective of spiritual masculinity is firm and challenging at times but, with love, is easily received. I believe men will be able to recalibrate their relationship with God and their loved ones!

Although he is no longer stalking the opposing team and coaching young men to be the best they can be, Jim is now walking in his calling, coaching men to be back to our original design."

—Ricky Sailor,
founder of Unsigned Preps and sports agent

"*Masculinity by Design* was written by a man for men. So, why is a woman endorsing it? Men, you may not know this, but your wife and children are your biggest cheerleaders. We truly, wholeheartedly, want you to succeed as husbands and fathers, to be the loving head of households God intended you to be. Jim Bradford, and more importantly, God, has this same desire for you!

So, wives, give *Masculinity by Design* to your man, in love, then allow him to read it on his own time and in his own way. Author Jim Bradford does not hold back, and your man will need intimate time with God for conversations that are specific to him. Allow God to inspire your husband, not you, through this process.

Men, if you read this book with an open heart and great humility, it will be life changing! Jim Bradford shares his own life experiences, successes, and failures, both as a provider and as head of his household. He asks questions to get you to think and offers scripture so you'll know his message is God-inspired. Find time with this book. Read it slowly. Meditate. Reflect. Then share with your family how God is speaking to you. Your wife and your children will love you for that! And as Jim would say, 'Blessings on your journey.'"

—Lori Marett,
author, screenwriter, editor, and mentor

"Jim Bradford is a leader of men. Through his testimony, he has exemplified how men can cultivate the position of father, husband, son, and spiritual leader. *Masculinity by Design* is a powerful, direct, and real guide for those men who do not want to settle and who desire to create a legacy of becoming a godly man."

—David Wilson,
pastor, men's groups coordinator,
Bayside Community Church

"It was an honor and privilege to read this book. The timing could not have been more perfect. Holy Spirit has been speaking these truths into my life again in a fresh and powerful way. It was a cleansing and convicting word that brought me to a renewed place of consecration of my life as a man, a husband, a father, and a grandfather. But also I was inspired to be a better bride to My Husband and My Lord! This is a word to bring forth and reveal all the 'Sons of God!' (Romans 8:19)."

—Daniel Dunn,
missionary in Poland, cofounder of
Because of Love International Ministry,
founding pastor of Real Life Church, Tampa

"God's hand and anointing are reflected in these Christian stories and biblical truths. *Masculinity by Design: Finding True North* brings light to a very dark world and will encourage those who have lost faith in the family. The clarity, insight, and passion once lost and now restored is a true testimony of how God creates beauty from ashes. The scripture and profound reflections will challenge not only husbands but wives as well. I believe these prophetic words will inspire generations to come."

—Rev. Carman Wuebbels,
pastor of Congregational Care and Missions
at Christ Church

"Very timely book! The image of what a man is can be increasingly confusing these days. I have had the honor of knowing Jim personally and getting to walk alongside him in his journey. Jim is always 100% real and raw. This book is from his heart and his passion for helping men find our way back to the design God had forged in our DNA. Jim has been through the trenches and is battle tested! This book isn't written from the perspective of sitting on the sidelines with a bunch of theories. Jim lays it all out there to bring honor and glory to God Almighty. Jim exemplifies a man pursuing God daily to be the best man, husband, father, business owner, and friend that he can be! Excited to see this book help other men on their own personal journey."

—Bob Spraker,
men's leadership team at Illuminate Church,
brother in Christ

"*Masculinity by Design* by my friend Jim Bradford wasn't just an eye-opening read, it was an example of how to recognize yourself and understand how to make important decisions through guidance and a personal walk with God. It's a life lesson on so many levels and how we are responsible for the choices we make. Life is tough and will test us all, as you know. This is a book offering guidance to the truth about masculinity. One man's road of working out his salvation through choices. You will have to check yourself along the way, and part of the lesson here is understanding that's what you should be doing. You will find yourself looking back through the book as a reference and a personal guide! I'm already looking forward to Jim's next book, and I think you will be too!"

—Chris Barton,
personal trainer, lifelong friend

"While James W. Bradford has a heart and gift for speaking into the lives of men, *Masculinity by Design: Finding True North* is really for everyone. James allows himself to become vulnerable by sharing deeply personal experiences and what he has learned as a result of both triumph and pain. It's real, it's raw, and he doesn't hold back. I can't remember a time where I circled, underlined, or highlighted in one book so much. I will use it as a reference so I don't forget all the things that impacted me, and I will share what I have learned with my boys as they grow. It should be required reading for anyone holding a 'man card.'"

—Lyle Gudmunsen,
husband, father, director/oil and gas professional,
singer/songwriter

"Timely. Necessary. Vital information. Hard-hitting and to the point. Jim and Mindy Bradford have penned a much-needed work to help reestablish the role of men in the family. In a world where the hierarchy God set in place is being stomped flat, this book helps reawaken the hearts of men, their value, and their role as the spiritual guide and example in their families. *Masculinity by Design* uses scripture, common sense, and prayer to motivate and revive the role of men. A must-read not only for men but for women as well—as the design God has put into motion comes to life."

—Cindy K. Sproles, best-selling,
award-winning author of *Meet Me Where I Am,
Lord* and *What Momma Left Behind*

"*Masculinity by Design* is a wake-up call for all dads. But this wake-up call isn't a loud, blaring alarm screaming in your ear. Jim Bradford communicates in a way that allows your heart and soul to be brought to life through profound teaching that regular guys need. He includes powerful insight on why men get stuck and a truly hopeful path forward. You can do this. Jim's riveting story is living proof."

—Tim Ingram,
lead pastor of Illuminate Church,
Celebration, Florida

MASCULINITY
by Design

Finding
True
North

seek the Designer

Honor the Designer

Matt 6. '33   *Mindy Bradford*

James W. Bradford with Mindy Bradford

Romans 8:28

**IRON
STREAM**

Birmingham, Alabama

Masculinity by Design

Iron Stream
An imprint of Iron Stream Media
100 Missionary Ridge
Birmingham, AL 35242
IronStreamMedia.com

Library of Congress Control Number: 2022914222

Cover design by Michelle Kenny

ISBN: 978-1-56309-623-5 (paperback)
ISBN: 978-1-56309-624-2 (e-book)

1 2 3 4 5—27 26 25 24 23

To the men fighting a fight that no one knows about. While privately battling thoughts of failure, you continue to climb the mountain of life. I want you to know that you are not alone. This book will give you hope, and your best days are yet to come.

CONTENTS

FOREWORD

This book is my brother's life story and message that I have had the honor and privilege of having a front-row seat to watch God write.

As with all people, our life stories are shaped by our experiences and the people God has allowed into our lives. God never wants us to waste any of our experiences but to learn from them and pass on what we have learned where others may benefit from them.

This book has been written to do just that, to share some life lessons learned from the school of hard knocks. It is smart to learn from your own life lessons; it is wise to learn from others.

What qualifies me, Elaine Roberts, to write this foreword and recommend that you read this book? As one of Jim's older sisters, I have been an eyewitness to his life since his birth and can validate every word and experience written in these pages. I have been a Christ follower for fifty-two years; a member of Saddleback Church in Lake Forest, California, for thirty-four years, sitting under the teaching and leadership of Rick

Warren; and on staff at Saddleback Church as a children's minister for the past twenty-two years and still going strong in God's call on my life to reach the next generation for Christ.

Why should you, the reader, make time to read a story by someone unknown, ordinary, and not famous? Because that is the category that most of us fit in! Our lives matter to God, and we learn from one another. This is an opportunity to learn from someone just like yourself! Your life matters to God. He wants to speak to you through this ordinary, everyday man to transform your life, which will transform your relationships. The fact you have picked up this book says you care about who you are and how you are living. Thank you for being open to becoming more of who God created you to be: like Him.

Elaine Roberts
Saddleback Church staff children's minister

PREFACE

In the beginning, God said, "Let there be light." Jesus told us the first thing we should do is seek God's kingdom. Seeking God's kingdom means seeking the light. The purpose of this book is to illuminate the dark places in our lives. We don't need another pep rally. We don't need another self-help book, and we don't need another checklist that we fail to complete. This book is neither a Bible study nor devotional. It is a call to return to God's design for manhood. The challenge to you is to allow God to shine in the rooms of your heart that you have not allowed anyone to see into. It's a look at biblical, foundational truths.

I once held these foundational truths near and dear to my heart. I walked in these truths for many years. Over time, I allowed trauma, pain, and disillusionment to pull me away. I found myself in darkness and crippled, where the enemy lives and thrives. I suffered deep wounds and still today carry scars from that time. Sadly, those I was called to set the example for and lead also suffered deep wounds. I don't want that for you, men.

Therefore, reading this book is more than just about your life. It's about those you have been called to care for, set the example for, lead, and protect.

I challenge you, men, to read the entire book. Allow it to do the work. The Holy Spirit will turn on the light, and it will shine brightly in the dark, hidden places. You will be tempted to stop reading and avoid the illumination. Do not give in! Press on. Keep reading, and find your way home. Find *True North*.

Jesus is the Light of the World. Let's walk in the light as He is in the light.

Blessings on your journey,
James W. Bradford

ACKNOWLEDGMENTS

To my sister, Elaine, you are my spiritual rock and mentor. Your influence, leadership, and prayers continue to shape my life. This book began with my phone call to you. Thank you, Sis.

To my best friend, Chris, you and your father gave me the first glimpse into a dynamic father-child relationship. I am forever grateful for your unconditional love, support, and belief in me for over thirty-five years. Words cannot adequately express my love for you.

To my daughters, Rachel, Amanda, and Karissa, my love for you and our relationship is what pushed me to seek out the truths in this book. The epic memories we share are legendary. Being your dad will always be my mountaintop experience. I love you more than you will ever know.

To Ricky, I am humbled and honored that you allowed me to experience a father-son relationship. Your impact cannot be measured. Your belief in me pushed me to seek Jesus with my whole heart. I'm so proud of you.

To Dan, you introduced me to the gospel of grace and the Father-Heart of God. While you pastored me, you planted the seeds for this book. I am forever grateful.

To Bob, your honesty, transparency, and willingness to get up before the crack of dawn to walk the road with a broken brother, facilitated this entire process. Thank you for allowing me to just be me. I love you, brother.

To my dearest Mindy, you breathed life into these dry bones. You took the passion of my heart and turned it into words. You believed in me and in this message. You have loved me with a supernatural love and shown me how incredible God's Design for Marriage can be.

To Lori, we were completely out of our element at the writers' conference. You took the time to listen to the message and believe in us. Your words of encouragement, support, and belief gave us the strength to move forward. Thank you.

To Suzanne, you sat with two novice writers and heard our heart. You were willing to take a risk. You listened and embraced the paradigm shift for godly manhood. Thank you for your courage.

To Cindy, your wisdom and guidance turned a bunch of bullet points into a flowing manuscript. Your combination of strength and grace was exactly what we needed, and a picture of Jesus. Thank you for mentoring us through the process.

To John Herring, we are forever grateful for your ability to look at the heart of the message instead of the credentials for the message. We look forward to walking shoulder-to-shoulder with you impacting the kingdom of God.

Design
Misrepresented

CHAPTER 1

THE CROSSROADS

Since the dawn of time, every man has visited the same crossroad in life. Some get there sooner than others, but eventually, we all ponder the same elusive questions: "How did I get here?" "Why am I here?" "Does it all really matter?" "Is God real, and what is the deal with this Jesus guy?"

My visitation to that crossroad was in 1991. I was twenty-one years old, sitting in the back of a pancake house, the only patron in that section. I was eating my breakfast and had to come to terms with some hard-to-accept truths. I realized I would never be a professional athlete. My football days were long gone.

Despite being gifted academically, I was an atrocious college student. I needed to come up with a game plan for my life. My desire was to figure out a way to stay in athletics and still earn a nice income. So, I devised a plan to attend law school and become a sports agent in the NFL. I was confident with my ability that I could pull this off if I applied myself. This would check all the boxes. Going down this road would allow me to stay connected to football.

As I sat there pondering all the events that needed to take place, I wrestled with the concept of God and Jesus. I had never attended church in my entire life. Two men came into the restaurant and sat at the table beside me. I sat there day-dreaming about my future but couldn't help but overhear them talking about Jesus. The passion and conviction in their voices were striking. I sat there listening to them for nearly five minutes. Astonished and mesmerized by their words, I got up to leave but stopped to ask them a question.

"How is your faith so strong?"

"What's your name?" They asked. "Why don't you sit down, Jim, and let's talk." During our conversation, we bounced back and forth between the subjects of Jesus and life in general.

"What are your goals and dreams?" they inquired.

"I want to go to law school and become a sports agent in the NFL."

The men looked at each other with a slight smirk.

The gentleman on my left said, "Well, I am an attorney." Then he looked to his friend and said, "Tell him what you do."

The man on my right said, "I am the chaplain for the Washington Redskins."

At that point, it became abundantly clear to me God was real. They shared several basic scriptures and prayed with me as I affirmed Jesus is the Way, the Truth, and the Life. That day, I accepted Jesus Christ as my Lord and Savior. Like most new believers, I took off running. I was filled with excitement and passion for this new life. However, I had a significant disconnect right out of the gate. I could only pray to Jesus.

In high school, the team joined together in the Lord's Prayer after our practices and games. I was well aware of the concept of praying to God as Father. I knew Jesus taught us to pray this way, but I just couldn't do it, without shutting down emotionally. Reciting the Lord's Prayer as a group was easy because it was impersonal. Now that prayer had become real, I could not pray to the Father, because my earthly father ruled with an iron fist. His presence was violent and fearful. He was a ticking time bomb. My perception of fatherhood was tragically impacted and warped. This was a deep wound, and I call it the *father wound*.

Theologically, I understood Jesus was God the Father in the flesh. However, praying to the Father was not an option for me. I only prayed to Jesus. I brushed it off as no big deal. This continued until my oldest daughter, Rachel, was conceived. The news of her forthcoming arrival was overwhelming, and a sense of unconditional love flooded over me. The weight of responsibility to care for her was not a burden but a joy. This was my chance to be something my biological father was not. I was going to be a dad.

Then it hit me. Is this how God feels about me? My intellectual mind grasped the concept, but the fears and emotions that surfaced about my father were deeply ingrained in my subconscious. The human brain is the ultimate digital recorder. From my infancy until his death, I witnessed a lifestyle of toxic attitudes and unacceptable behaviors.

Consequently, my subconscious mind created an image of fatherhood from those experiences. We naturally view God the Father through the prism of our earthly father. I transposed my biological father's character and behaviors onto God the Father. What is your father wound?

Was your father physically there but not present? Was it impossible to earn his approval? Was he absent from your life, or did he abuse you? Do you even know him? What character traits from your earthly father have you subconsciously transposed onto the heavenly Father?

The reality as Christian men is our persona takes on even greater importance as we endeavor to model godly behaviors to those around us. We represent the heart of God as Father to our wives, children, coworkers, and those with whom we interact.

We must answer this piercing question: Are we representing God's heart accurately? My father horribly misrepresented the image of God, which led to my quest to know the *Father-Heart* of God. As a result, I grew up with no clear understanding of what a good father should be. I became very aware of the chasm between the lives I had witnessed from my father and from other men I was around, versus the life scripture calls us to live. It burned in me like fire in my bones to represent God accurately to my wife, children, and those who came in contact with me.

> *Are we representing God's heart accurately?*

One day while reading the Old Testament, I noticed a theme among many of the kings who were considered good kings. They loved God with their whole heart, yet many of their children became evil and did not obey God. It was both confusing and terrifying. A pattern became evident as I continued my research. Many of these kings tolerated and/or worshipped at the high places (places of worship of the pagan gods) in their kingdoms. As a result, their children could not see their fathers' hearts and inward devotion to God.

All they saw was their external behaviors. These actions sent a mixed message to their children about being devoted to God.

This struck me to my core as a soon-to-be father. It led me on a journey to fully seek and understand the words Philip spoke to Jesus when he said, "Show us the Father" (John 14:8–9). Jesus responded, "[Anyone] who has seen Me has seen the Father." This challenged me to truly seek the *Father-Heart* of God.

When I began this journey, I tried to be everything my earthly father was not. I wanted to be the best possible husband and dad. What I learned through the process was pursuing God's design for manhood was *not* to make me a better man.

So, I challenge you not to view this as a self-help book. The purpose is to *know* the *Father-Heart* of God experientially. The purpose of the pursuit is so we can manifest His heart in our daily lives—to be seen by those with whom we come in contact. Don't get hung up on pursuing the fruit. Focus on pursuing the root. Being a better husband, father, disciple, and human being is a by-product of this endeavor.

Through this process, I discovered a threefold responsibility of men, which included being (1) an *Image-Bearer* of the Father, (2) a *disciple* of Jesus, and (3) the Bride of Christ. For those who are fathers, it is our calling to *model* biblical principles, be supportive through *affirmation*, and appropriately *discipline* our children. As I continued to search, I pleaded with God to teach me more about who He is and show me how to be the same father-dad to my daughter that He is to me.

If you have never fully known Abba God and His *Father-Heart*, then this study will help you understand God as your dad, so you can accurately portray *His heart* to everyone in your life. As we dig deeper into these concepts, we will explore living a life of discipleship and understanding what it means to be the Bride of Christ. Until you understand these truths, you are not truly free from a distorted view of God. Discovering the true image of Abba Father will lead to *freedom*. *Freedom* starts *NOW!*

Blessings on your journey.

CHAPTER 2

A FORK IN THE ROAD

Raised in a lower-income, blended family in the Tampa Bay area and as the youngest of eight children, I was enveloped in extreme dysfunction—alcoholism and physical, emotional, and verbal abuse. I excelled in school and was popular among my peers despite this environment. My father was abusive, taking out his wrath on my mother, siblings, and myself daily. My concept of being a father grew skewed from an early age, and I longed for a safe and happy home life.

As an elementary school kid, not only was I exposed to physical violence and verbal abuse, but also the false representation of manhood went to a whole new level. When I was a first-grader, my dad would take me to the mechanic shop for his weekly poker game with the guys. My memories of these trips included the smell of machine oil lingering in the air as we walked past nude poster pin-ups on the walls. This started shaping my psyche that portrayed women simply as objects for pleasure rather than as people.

This theme continued, and when I was in third grade, I found the not-so-private hiding place for pornography in our home, which happened to be tucked away in my bedroom. There were stacks of magazines available for regular viewing. As a child, I had no idea the damage I was doing by repeatedly viewing these pictures.

The vulgar jokes I heard at the auto body shop gave words to the images in my mind. Despite being so young, I understood at a much deeper level. It was commonplace for the men in my life to speak vulgarities about women and make horrific sexual gestures toward them in my presence.

For us, a typical weekend consisted of the family attending my Little League games, where I usually played very well. Our team frequently won. In those moments, life was wonderful because my father was verbally supportive and proud of my achievement. Upon our return home, my dad would become highly intoxicated, which led to an intense fight with Mother, resulting in him beating her up in my presence.

My older brothers tried to step in occasionally, but Dad would turn his wrath on them. My father was a paradox. He was firm on me moralistically, as he instilled the qualities of respectfulness and treating others well. However, he did not reflect any of those character traits in his own life. I quickly learned how to stay in my father's good graces by demonstrating athletic achievement, being popular with the girls, and having good grades in school.

In my teen years, I turned to athletics to find a sense of approval from others and my father. Before long, I discovered I excelled in sports. I developed my sense of identity around athleticism, popularity, bodybuilding, and powerlifting. This fed my need for approval from others. The false identity for true manhood had already taken root. The belief system that real men were athletic, promiscuous, and strong had a firm grip on my identity.

On a quest to earn my father's approval through athletic achievement, I joined a local gym that happened to be one of the best training gyms for powerlifters in the United States. I met several men here, hopeful they could help me become the man I longed to be—at least, what I thought a man *should* be.

I have no memory of ever attending church or even hearing about Jesus, so I was incredibly conflicted in my feelings, especially with the relationship with my father. He not only attended every game but attended every practice, as well. He robustly communicated his pride in me and my accomplishments, whether on the field or in the weight room. That made me feel valued. However, I absolutely disdained the brutal abuse I witnessed daily toward us at home.

In 1981, when I was a sophomore in high school, my father died from complications resulting from an aneurism. A part of me was glad he was gone. When he died, his atrocious behavior died with him. Unfortunately, so did the feelings of approval and acceptance I earned from him. Looking back, this unconsciously pushed me even harder to perform in the areas where I sought approval—the weight room and sports, as well as popularity among my peers and a promiscuous lifestyle.

By the time I was a senior in high school, I had begun to excel in weightlifting. I even competed in the Teenage Mr. Florida Bodybuilding Contest. After graduating high school, I went to college to play football.

I felt confident about myself as a man, athlete, and student. After all, school was easy for me. Sports were my passion, popularity followed me, and I was the second strongest guy on the team, even as a college freshman. That is when things began to unravel. I stopped attending class and was either at a party or in the weight room. I was eventually cut from the college football team and expelled for failing grades. Although completely capable, I made little effort and rarely attended class. In my cockiness, I assumed I could fly through academics the way I had during elementary and high school. I was wrong and absolutely gutted.

For the first time in my life, I experienced failure and total humiliation. The shining star had crashed and burned. When I returned home, I went to my local gym. The guys there noticed I was in great shape. They began to encourage and motivate me back into competitive bodybuilding. The Mr. Tampa Bodybuilding Contest was seven weeks away, and this was my opportunity to regain self-confidence as a man through athletic success and achievement. My training went so well that I not only entered the Mr. Teenage Tampa Bodybuilding Contest, but also entered the men's division, Mr. Tampa Bodybuilding Contest. I won first place in the teenage division and received second place to my training partner in the men's division, who was the overall winner. For a teenager to place second in the men's division was a significant achievement, and I felt a sense of approval and accomplishment. My self-esteem was restored. At least, I thought it was.

During the next year and a half, I suffered several significant injuries that made me realize competitive bodybuilding was off the table. Lost, confused, and trying to find my identity as a man, I turned to the military. I excelled in the army and won Soldier of the Cycle upon completing basic training.

Thousands of people attended the graduation ceremony, including friends and family members of those who had completed basic training. Yet, as I was awarded the medal for being the best trainee on the base, not one person was there to celebrate my accomplishment. It was a bittersweet day. I knew if my father were alive, he would have been there. I longed for my father's encouraging words but was conflicted and disgusted that I wanted to hear from him because of what he had done to our family.

During my time in the army, I began to read the Bible, and I longed for a family. Not just *any* family, but a *good* family. Upon graduation from basic training, my first duty station was in Germany. Shortly after I arrived, I met Chris Barton, a fellow soldier. We became best friends and training partners at the gym. The two of us were inseparable. He talked about his love and respect for his father in a way I had never before heard. I remember thinking that I hoped my children would someday talk about me that way because I knew I didn't feel that way about my father. I wanted to do it differently.

After serving for two years, we took a fourteen-day leave to Texas to visit with Chris's parents. Watching his dad interact with his mother was a huge culture shift for me. His dad was kind, gentle, uplifting, and treated Chris's mother like a queen. Mr. Barton gave me the first picture of the type of father and husband I wanted to become.

Chris's dad was a strong Christian. I did not know the Lord at the time, so I could not connect the dots to understand why he was the man he was. I had no concept of what a Christian looked like. Thinking back on this event, I realized God had planted the seed in me to someday become a godly man in my home.

> *God had planted the seed in me to someday become a godly man in my home.*

Following the trip to Texas, I desperately wanted a family that would share happiness, love, safety, and fun. I realized the army life was not conducive to my desired family life. Despite being successful in the army, I knew I needed to return to civilian life when my term ended.

To say I struggled when I returned to civilian life is an understatement. I fell into all the old habits and empty pleasures of my youth. My life consisted of going to the gym during the day and nightclubs in the evenings, and all of the destructive behaviors that accompanied that lifestyle. From the beginning, my moral compass was broken. I did not have a *True North* to guide me through life as a man.

CHAPTER 3

GOD THE FATHER SHOWS HIMSELF

After the life-changing encounter at the pancake house, I returned to my apartment and called my sister, Elaine. She was a rock in the family and a strong Christian. I shared with her everything that had just transpired.

"Jim, you need to come to visit for a while. Let me help you get your spiritual legs under you." She was incredibly excited, and I accepted her invitation to come and stay with her for a couple of weeks. Elaine attended Saddleback Church with Pastor Rick Warren in California, so I visited with her. I had never really experienced being in a church, and listening to Pastor Rick teach was amazing. After a few weeks of going through some basic Christian faith concepts with my sister, I returned home. My longing for a wife and family grew even stronger. I wanted to love and be loved.

A few weeks later, I met the woman I would later marry. We had a very similar childhood, and she was a competitive bodybuilder. Our commitment was to have God at the center of our relationship. However, neither of us grasped the full concept. We both knew the lives we once lived did nothing but hurt us, and we wanted something better. We dated and soon married.

After we married, we found a church in Tampa similar to Saddleback Church and immediately became involved. Unfortunately, several red flags appeared in my relationship with my wife. I felt disconnected from her, and this pushed me to pursue God even more. As a result, I had a passion for spending time in prayer and studying God's Word. I fully immersed myself in a spiritual walk with the Lord. This burning desire for a healthy, loving family forced me to gravitate toward children and youth ministries. I volunteered numerous hours to help, aware of God's nudge and call on my life to enter the ministry.

As we became involved with the church and attended potlucks and other events, it became obvious I easily connected with the children and teens in our church. After several months of observations by the elders, they approached me about teaching Sunday school. I gladly accepted. I thoroughly enjoyed teaching children Bible stories, and they loved my energy and authenticity. About one year after I started teaching Sunday school, the church announced it would be hiring a new youth pastor. Privately, I desperately wanted this job.

One month before the announcement of this vacancy, I was at a revival service in another city. At the end of the service, I went forward in response to the altar call for those who desired to go into full-time ministry.

At the altar, I wept, saying, "Lord, send me," reciting Isaiah 6. In my mind, I was visualizing the scene when God asked, "Whom shall I send?" In the passage, Isaiah responded, "Send me." Not only did I pray at the altar that evening, but it was already a regular part of my daily devotion and prayer life.

Once the church announced its search for a full-time youth pastor, my heart filled with hope that this may actually happen. I hadn't told anyone about my experience at the revival or of my personal prayers about pursuing full-time ministry. Because of my involvement with the church, I had become good friends with the elders. I wanted to make sure this call to be the youth pastor was God's will for my life. Therefore, I did not speak a word to the elders about my interest in the position. I did not want the position given to me due to my relationships with them.

In my prayer life, I told God, "If this is Your will, they have to come to me." This happened in February 1994. By mid-May, the eldership called and scheduled a meeting with me. They told me they did not have peace about any of the applicants interviewed for the position. They revealed that God laid on their hearts I was supposed to be the next youth pastor.

"Are you interested in becoming our next youth pastor?"

"Are you kidding me? I have been praying for this for almost six months. Yes, I would love to be your next youth pastor!" I said.

We hugged and prayed together, and it was an incredible moment. The senior pastor set my ordination date for July 3.

On the morning of July 3, my ordination day, I woke up and opened my devotional, and it was Isaiah 6. I was stunned. The exact passage I had been praying for six months about full-time ministry was the scripture for my devotion on the day I was ordained. I felt my heavenly Father had made it plain I was on the right path, and He had plans for me.

During this time, my wife became pregnant with our first child. I was overcome by fear and doubt about how to be a father. All I knew was I wanted to do everything the complete opposite of my earthly father. That sent me on a quest of crying out to God.

"Teach me, oh God, how to be a father, and a dad, the way You are to me."

During this time of studying the Old Testament, I noticed a pattern with the kings of Israel. I discovered many of the kings who were good, loved, and served God with their whole hearts had children who did not serve or walk with the Lord. Terrified, I cried out to God, "Do not let this be in my life, God!"

Focused on these kings, I pressed into the point, through prayer and study, and noticed they did not tear down all the high places of their kingdoms. I concluded the children of these kings could not see the sincerity of faith and love for the God of their fathers. They could only see the duplicity in their fathers' actions by saying they loved God while still worshipping at the high places. Is it possible, then, that these mixed messages caused the children to reject their fathers' God because of the duplicity in their words and behaviors?

It became clear to me how critically important it was that my beliefs, words, and actions were in alignment with one another for my children to witness. My study took me to the words Jesus spoke about himself. Jesus told us when we see Him, we've seen the Father. He also said, "Peace be with you! As the Father has sent me, I am sending you" (John 20:21 NIV). I realized the mandate on my life was to demonstrate for my children the heart and love of the Father in the same way Jesus demonstrated God's heart and love for me.

Running parallel to my passion to be the father to my children I had never known in my youth was a deep desire to have a radiant, Christian marriage—one filled with passionate, unconditional love. I had heard people talk about marriages such as this but hadn't personally experienced it for myself. Outwardly, our marriage looked good. We had all the external, Christian behaviors that made for a good marriage, but inwardly it was extremely broken. It was void of deep, meaningful conversation, healthy intimacy, and spiritual unity.

While I was studying the book of Hosea, the Lord opened my eyes to understanding the husband/wife relationship, which is a prophetic foreshadowing of the relationship between Jesus and the church. Hosea represented Jesus whereas Gomer represented the church, or the Bride. As a Christian man, I realized I was called to love my wife the way Jesus loved the church, as reflected in the story of Hosea. I am called to model the passion and unconditional love that Jesus has for His Bride, the church, to my wife.

During this same time, Tony Dungy was the head coach for the Tampa Bay Buccaneers. His influence in the Tampa Bay area, to both Christians and non-Christians alike, cannot be overstated. He was so influential that most of the Christian men I knew wanted to be just like Coach Dungy, myself included. He was an incredible male role model and coach, exemplifying his strength through self-control, gentleness, and kindness. Furthermore, he was not ashamed of the gospel of Jesus Christ and shared the reality of his faith humbly in a very public way. His book *Quiet Strength* forever impacted my perspective on manhood.

On July 3, 1994, I was ordained and became a full-time youth pastor. The call on my life was real, and I was sold out to being the best youth pastor and representative for Jesus I could be. As my church's youth pastor, I was responsible for all youth, from elementary school to college-aged students.

The parents of my youth groups regularly asked me questions regarding how to discipline their children and teenagers. At this time, Dr. James Dobson had two books, *The Strong-Willed Child* and *Dare to Discipline*, which were very popular and a big topic of discussion in the 1990s. Again, my mission led me on another quest, this time to research the subject of discipline.

Since I had joined the staff at my local church, it seemed only natural to spend time with the members of my youth group in the same places they were spending their time. I became heavily involved in the local high school athletics department. God opened the door for me, and I was hired part-time as a football coach, as well as being designated the team chaplain. During this period, I became very aware of the coaches' words toward their athletes. Though some of their words were positive and motivating, equally as many were damaging personal insults that humiliated the students. At the same time, my senses heightened to the way many of the parents spoke to their children. Sadly, there were many similarities. It became clear why some of the teens were acting out inappropriate behaviors. They were confirming and living up to the condition of their heart. Solomon is emphatic in Proverbs about the power of words. "Above all else, guard your heart, for everything you do flows from it" (Proverbs 4:23 NIV). I started to see the *power* of words,

> The concept of being a father who represented God's heart encompassed three equal parts: modeling, affirmation, and discipline.

as stated in Proverbs 18:21 (NIV): "The tongue has the power of life and death, and those who love it will eat its fruit."

This realization led me to understand the importance of affirmation, which, according to *Merriam-Webster Dictionary*, is "an act of saying or showing that something is true." For the remainder of this book, our focus on the word *affirmation* primarily relates to the words we use and their powerful effect on a person's heart. Eventually, the shaping of the heart becomes our identity.

After contemplating all of my newly discovered knowledge, the concept of being a father who represented God's heart encompassed three equal parts: modeling, affirmation, and discipline. Upon further reflection, I noticed it represented the Triune Godhead of the Father, Son, and Holy Spirit. My eyes were opened, and I observed the following: Jesus is our model, the Holy Spirit is our affirmer, and God the Father is our disciplinarian. Hebrews 12:4–11 (NIV) states:

> In your struggle against sin, you have not yet resisted to the point of shedding your blood. And have you completely forgotten this word of encouragement that addresses you as a father addresses his son? It says,
>
> "My son, do not make light of the Lord's discipline,
>   and do not lose heart when he rebukes you,
> because the Lord disciplines the one he loves,
>   and he chastens everyone he accepts as his son."
>
> Endure hardship as discipline; God is treating you as his children. For what children are not disciplined by their father? If you are not disciplined—and

everyone undergoes discipline—then you are not legitimate, not true sons and daughters at all. Moreover, we have all had human fathers who disciplined us and we respected them for it. How much more should we submit to the Father of spirits and live! They disciplined us for a little while as they thought best; but God disciplines us for our good, in order that we may share in his holiness. No discipline seems pleasant at the time, but painful. Later on, however, it produces a harvest of righteousness and peace for those who have been trained by it.

A light bulb went off. To represent God to my family and the others around me, I had to model all three concepts: Modeling, Affirmation, and Discipline, or M.A.D. I told myself, "Jim, it's time to get M.A.D. and stay M.A.D.!"

Designed to Be an *Image-Bearer*

CHAPTER 4

GET M.A.D., STAY M.A.D.

As we begin our journey living according to the design and walk as an *Image-Bearer*, it is important we do some house-cleaning and clear up a few common misperceptions.

This journey *should not* be undertaken in order to:

- Get your wife to love you.
- Get your children to obey you.
- Get people to respect you.
- Or be viewed in a positive light by society.

Jesus, the perfect *Image-Bearer*, modeled how to be the *Image-Bearer* of the Father. Even so, He was still doubted by some of His own townspeople. Others mocked, scoffed, rejected, and betrayed Jesus, and eventually, the religious leaders had Him crucified. Many of society, then and now, do not believe Jesus was who He said He was—the Son of the Living God.

If the measuring stick for success was a behavioral change and the acceptance of Jesus by those around Him, then He was an utter failure. To know God intimately and for others to see Him in us is what we are seeking. How people respond to us is not relevant to our pursuit.

That being said, we must be prepared to give ourselves grace. This road is narrow and can be difficult. Often, our behavior does not reflect God's perfect love in our lives. At times, we misrepresent Him and even ignore His teachings. Furthermore, it does not change the reality of who God is or how He loves us and longs to have a relationship with us. Romans 5:8 (ESV) tells us, "God shows his love for us in that while we were still sinners, Christ died for us."

> *To know God intimately and for others to see Him in us is what we are seeking.*

Therefore, His perfect love for us is not connected to our response to it. John echoed what Paul is saying here when He stated, "We love Him because He first loved us" (1 John 4:19). So, on the days you feel lost or struggling, knowing Jesus first loved you must be your *True North*, the place where you return to find your way home.

When I first understood how God demonstrated His love for me, it was incredibly liberating as a husband and a father.

Men, do we want our spouses to love and respect us? Yes. Do we want our children to obey us? Of course, we do. But we must understand it is not about us doing things in an attempt to modify or change the behaviors of others. It is simply to allow God to manifest Himself through us in our daily lives.

As we dig deeper into the concept of being an *Image-Bearer*, I want to set the road map for where we are going. While awaiting the birth of my oldest daughter, Rachel, I struggled with the responsibility of fatherhood. I desired to be the best father I could possibly be, though keenly aware of the negative impression my earthly father's behavior had on me.

As we look into the life of Jesus as our example, we will deal with spiritual principles. Jesus was not only the Son of God but also the Son of Man. On this journey of being a tangible representation of Jesus, we will intently look at His life as a laborer, employee, and a man who enjoyed life with His friends. Since Jesus is our role model, He is our *True North*. When we veer off course, we must look at our compass to get back on the right track. Remember, God promises to give grace to the humble, so let's pursue this with a teachable spirit.

CHAPTER 5

M—MODELING

While I was in the army, part of my training was called *land navigation*. The drill sergeants dropped us off in the middle of the forest with a compass. We had to find our way out of it. The first thing that we had to do was determine where we were. If we didn't know where our journey began, we would not be able to make it to our destination. The GPS systems we use in our world today work in much the same way. We key in our destination, but before it starts to map the directions, it asks about our starting location. Knowing your starting location is critical.

Since we know our design as humans is broken by original sin, our own perspective and paradigm may feel like *True North*, but it is not *True North*. It is critical to understand our role as *Image-Bearer* accurately. Like a compass, if it is off the slightest degree, the longer you travel, the further off-course you will become.

One of the things I love about living in Florida is being able to play golf year-round. The PGA Tour has a Father and Son tournament just outside of Orlando every year. It is an incredible tournament to watch, as we see some of the greatest golf legends take the course with their sons and daughters. One of the best parts about watching the tournament is noticing the simi-

Since we know our design as humans is broken by original sin, our own perspective and paradigm may feel like True North, but it is not True North.

larities of a child in his body movements, gestures, idiosyncrasies, and facial expressions, compared to his parent. In fact, the commentators spend a significant amount of time talking about how they see younger, living clones of the dads on the golf course.

I remember chuckling about this as I watched these fathers and sons. Then I began to look at my daughters. Suffice it to say, I was surprised by how similar their personal traits and daily life looked to mine. Unfortunately, that included some of my negative character traits, as well. Upon further reflection, I asked myself, "How much effort or energy did I put into getting my daughters to do those things?"

The answer was zero. The reason pro golfers and their children look so similar in their nuances and body language, and the reason my daughters displayed some of my own character traits, is simply because we consistently modeled those behaviors in our relationships with them. Over time, they became ingrained behaviors and characteristics in our children's lives.

Take a moment to reflect on your childhood. Do you see any of your parents' negative character traits manifested in your life? How about your children? Do they respond in similar ways to you in positive or negative situations? If so, the question for you is, which father are you emulating? The First Adam, in the Garden, or the Second Adam, Jesus?

It leads me to question myself further: "Where did I learn my subconscious and internal behaviors? What model am I following? Is it my perspective of what manhood looks like? Is it possible I have a mixture of worldly and spiritual views? Or is it just a natural outflow of people, perspectives, or ideas from my own life?" Paul tells us in Romans 12:2 (NIV), "Do not conform to the pattern of this world, but be transformed by the renewing of your mind. Then you will be able to test and approve what God's will is—his good, pleasing and perfect will."

A Humble Servant

Jesus told His disciples, "If you really know me, you will know my Father as well" (John 14:7 NIV). Knowing and understanding Jesus is an essential component of being an *Image-Bearer* of the *Father-Heart* of God. Therefore, who is Jesus? John 1:1–4 tells us Jesus is literally God in the flesh. Paul stated in Philippians that Jesus appeared as a man, humbled Himself, and became obedient to death on a cross. Furthermore, Jesus Himself said, "For even the Son of Man did not come to be served, but to serve, and to give his life as a ransom for many" (Mark 10:45 NIV). As incredible as the sacrifice and death of Jesus on a cross was, He lived His life as a ransom prior to His being arrested in the Garden of Gethsemane, as well.

In my opinion, one of the greatest examples of this was on the last night Jesus was alive. After having supper with His disciples, Jesus washed their feet. Let's look at this event in greater detail to understand it in context.

In our modern world, we don't have a clear picture of what it meant to wash someone's feet as it was done in biblical times. Most people are aware this was considered a menial job, but let's be frank, people's feet were disgusting. Especially back then. There were wild goats, sheep, oxen, and other animals roaming around, and there would have been animal feces between people's toes and on the soles of their feet. For Jesus to be willing to wash their nasty feet, knowing He was the Son of God, along with all the struggles He faced with this ragtag group of followers, He still chose to humble Himself and be a servant to them.

Jesus had a mastery of the Old Testament scriptures. He knew what Isaiah 53 prophesied about the brutality of His forthcoming crucifixion. Yet, despite the fact Jesus knew He was about to face the most excruciating moments in His entire life, He still chose to make this supper, the last night together with His dearest friends, about serving them.

As if that were not impressive enough, we need to remind ourselves Judas was not yet exposed. Jesus treated him with the same incredible love and act of service as He did the others. His love and care for Judas had to have been on par with how He loved and treated every other disciple that night. When Jesus told them someone would betray Him, everyone was confused and had no idea who it would be. They all questioned themselves. Mark 14:19 tells us, "And they began to be sorrowful, and to say to Him one by one, '*Is* it I?' And another said, '*Is* it I?'"

Pause and take a moment to let the reality of that event sink deep into your mind. From their perspective, Jesus was larger than life. They had watched Him love the unlovely, teach with power and authority, challenge the religious mindset, and perform many miracles. At this moment, Jesus was serving all of them with an equal amount of love, and He had just revealed one of them would be His betrayer. James, Peter, and John were Jesus's inner circle, and they went with Him to the Mount of Transfiguration, yet all three wondered if they were this unknown betrayer.

The only way it makes sense is if Jesus interacted with and loved Judas in the same way He did James, John, and Peter. Jesus went on to expose Judas, telling him to do it quickly. My point to you is, how do you treat the Judas in your life? Do you offer grace and kindness or retaliation?

To apply this concept to my life as a husband and father, I must ask myself the following questions. Do I create a warm, loving environment in my home after having a hard day at work? Or do I allow a difficult day that I know is coming, much like Jesus's pending crucifixion, to poison the atmosphere of tonight? Do I make excuses, defend and justify my bad attitude, fits of rage, anger, or reclusiveness because I think nobody understands how hard I have it? Remember, Jesus told us in the same way the Father sent Him, He also sends us (John 20:21).

Men, we are commanded to grab a towel and a basin of water and humble ourselves as servants. Yes, we are commanded to wash feet and serve others despite the challenges in our own lives.

Furthermore, Paul states in 1 Corinthians 6:19–20 (NIV), "You are not your own; you were bought at a price." The reality is, I don't have a choice. If I want to accept the free gift of grace and forgiveness of my sins, then I have to surrender my life and be willing to allow God to shape me into a servant, like Jesus.

CHAPTER 6

MODELING PROVISION

For many of you, it is not the first time you have heard of or read something about the reality of Jesus being a servant, but that is only the tip of the iceberg. Before we go much deeper, let's put it into terms we can understand.

I am a father, a husband, a coworker, a business owner, a Christian, a friend, a brother, and a neighbor, yet I am simply a man.

There is only one of me, but to fully know me and who I am, you must know me as every one of the roles I bear in life. Likewise, there is only one God, but He has many different roles, or images, that He plays in our lives. When Jesus taught us how to pray, He said we should pray to God as, "Our Father, who is in heaven, Hallowed be Your name" (Matthew 6:9 AMP). Although there are many books written on the names of God, I want to look at a few of them that are most relevant to me as a husband and father.

One of the most popular names of God from the Old Testament is *Jehovah Jireh*. It means *The Lord is my Provider*. Many of us seem to gravitate to the name rather quickly and have a fairly strong faith when it comes to understanding who that part of God is. We recognize that apart from Him, we have nothing and can do nothing. It is easy to think of God the Provider for financial resources.

We say things like, "He owns the cattle on a thousand hills," or "The battle belongs to the Lord," because we recognize He is the provider for every good thing in life. Jesus said, "Anyone who has seen me has seen the Father" (John 14:9 NIV). He had to come here to be a living picture of Jehovah Jireh for us to fully grasp the meaning.

The most obvious place Jesus showed us and lived out that He was Jehovah Jireh was on the cross. He willingly *provided Himself* as the sacrifice for our sins. Remember, Jesus is God in the flesh. He knew the consequences of sin. He knew He would be beaten beyond human recognition. He knew He was innocent, but He also knew His innocence provided a way out for us. As incredibly powerful and amazing Jesus's life was, I want to look at some other areas of His life where He demonstrated provision on a practical level. At first glance, these next examples may not be as impressive as the cross, but they are equally meaningful and powerful demonstrations of Jehovah Jireh.

The Adulterous Woman

What about the woman caught in adultery? She was caught in the very act. The law of Moses said she should be stoned.

Jesus's response was remarkable. Unflustered by the intensity of the situation, He was able to empathize with the woman yet still discern the intentions of the zealots. I'm sure she wondered since she was caught in the act, "Where's the man?" Flushing out their true motives, Jesus revealed these accusers had neither an interest in the truth nor care for the public humiliation of the lady. They were simply trying to trap Jesus, but He cut to the core of the situation with these words: "He who is without sin among you, let him throw a stone at her first" (John 8:7).

It is essential not to read through this passage too quickly. In order to understand the real power behind what Jesus did, we must remember He could have stoned her and been justified, according to Moses's Law. Jesus was the only one standing there who was without sin. Therefore, the level of unconditional love, grace, and mercy that He *provided* for her at that moment is a fulfillment of Jehovah Jireh. Through this act, Jesus demonstrated how to provide for those in distress.

The Ten Lepers

How about the ten lepers? As we have become disconnected to the role of foot washer, we have also become disconnected from the concept of people with leprosy. This happens because we are far removed from biblical times. Consider the life of a leper. Try to envision being banished from other people, kept from the feel of human touch, or being void of interaction on a deep level, while constantly declaring you are unclean to the world. Not to mention that your body and your life are completely falling apart. Things are literally falling off. Thus, for Jesus to enter their world, make them feel clean, and touch and talk to them was a remarkable act of compassionate love for the sick and afflicted. Again, Jesus showed us how *The Lord Provides* by being Jehovah Jireh to the lepers.

The Woman Who Washed Jesus's Feet

Let's look at the prostitute who washed Jesus's feet with her tears. I want to shelf the fact that she was a prostitute for now and look at her as a person who got off course in life. The type of sin isn't relevant.

This story happened as part of Jesus's everyday life. He sat down for dinner with some of the religious leaders from the area. I would equate the religious leaders in this event to the people in our everyday lives—those who are successful by the world's standards and have it all together. Obviously, they had no room for this type of person in their lives, and they took it a step further by wondering why Jesus accommodated and welcomed her. I absolutely love how Jesus turned the tables on them.

He equated her extravagant expression of love with her comprehension of her need for much forgiveness. He then shined the light into their hearts. He told them the reason they had done nothing for Him since He arrived was their perceived lack of the need for forgiveness. For this woman, Jesus *provided* a safe place to find redemption, restoration, and healing. Again, Jesus, as Jehovah Jireh, saw her deepest need and modeled how to be a provider.

What I hope you see is that Jehovah Jireh is not limited to finances. It is much wider, deeper, and higher than we first realized.

The Good Samaritan

Now, let's look at the story of the Good Samaritan. This must have been one of the most radical, controversial, and provocative stories Jesus told. He was asked, "What must I do to inherit eternal life?" (Luke 10:25 NIV). The question is still important to most people today. To conclude Jesus's answer to this question, He told the story of the Good Samaritan. Surely, there must be important information in this parable to answer such a monumental question.

Jesus created a narrative to which everyone listening could relate, about a man traveling down a road. Everyone knew it was a famous yet dangerous road as "The Road of Blood." Take a moment and think about your city. What is the most dangerous area of your town? Envision yourself in it, and imagine a man naked, beaten, and nearly dead, struggling on this dangerous road. That's where we are. Also, there was a priest, a Levite, and a Samaritan.

Jesus did not pick these three people randomly. He was boldly proving a point with conviction. A priest and a Levite are both Jews, pure Jews. In fact, being a priest was about the highest honor a Jew could have. His role was to represent man to God and God to man. Being a Levite was not far behind, as they were to serve God's people (or God's children)

> *Our provision includes not only finances but also an environment of grace, mercy, protection, and safety, by embracing others in their weaknesses.*

with their entire lives. Then there is the Samaritan—from a group despised by Jews as being half-breeds—who is considered unclean and rejected by God. In today's vernacular, Samaritans were clearly victims of racism. For Jesus to make the Samaritan the hero of this story, and to expose the utter failure of those who were supposed to represent God, was even more radical than we can begin to comprehend. Our takeaway from this parable is to live a life like the Samaritan and provide a voice of justice for victims of racism.

The point I am trying to make by looking at the life of Jesus is, that we are called to be a provider. Our provision includes not only finances but also an environment of grace, mercy, protection, and safety, by embracing others in their weaknesses or time of need.

CHAPTER 7

MODELING PEACE

J ehovah Shalom means *The Lord is my Peace.* I own an air conditioning company in central Florida. It is pretty remarkable the amount of people who call in thinking the thermostat is their problem. They recognize how important that little device is. When it fails to function correctly, the atmosphere in the home gets unlivable very quickly. Years ago, as I worked on a thermostat, I began to chuckle.

"God made men to be thermostats. Unfortunately, many of us are just thermometers," I thought to myself.

Let's look at the difference between the two. A thermometer has one job. It simply tells us what the room's temperature is. The device is powerless to do anything else. It doesn't matter if it is hot or cold, it simply reports the facts of its environment. A thermostat is quite different. The thermostat has the ability to know the temperature of the room as well. It also has the power to turn the air conditioner on or off, as needed, in order to maintain the desired temperature.

After this epiphany, I became aware of conversations I had with other men over the next several weeks. It became evident that as I listened to my male friends talk about the *temperature* of their marriages, families, and life in general, they felt powerless to change it. They spoke as though they were victims in this hot room. We are not victims. We are *Image-Bearers*. God is *Jehovah Shalom*. He is our *Peace*. If I am to be an *Image-Bearer*, when I enter the room, peace should enter the room, regardless of the atmosphere of the room upon my entry. I should bring not only peace but also the peace that passes all understanding.

> **We are not victims. We are Image-Bearers. God is Jehovah Shalom. He is our Peace.**

I cannot overstate the importance of peace. It is imperative we are on the same page when we talk about it. *Peace is not* the absence of conflict or problems. Rather, *peace is* the presence of the Lord. Peace has a very important sidekick—joy. I like to view peace and joy as Power Twins.

They are the crime fighters of my mind and heart. Peace guards my heart, and joy protects my mind. Proverbs tells me the most important thing I can do is guard my heart because out of my heart flows my entire life. It also says what I think in my heart, I will become. To further stress its importance, Matthew 12:34 says, "For out of the abundance of the heart the mouth speaks," and I will eat of the fruit of my lips.

These truths are not just hyped-up spiritual talk. They have a very real effect on our natural lives. I experienced getting a sick heart in the most literal sense possible. In the summer of 2020, I finally hit rock bottom. I had suffered from inner turmoil for twenty-eight years, yet I still strove to walk in step with

Jesus. All the while, my life continued to be bombarded with disappointments and betrayals. I became disillusioned and lost my hope for a better future.

The year 2020 will be remembered as the year of COVID-19. But that year for me marked the culmination of years of brokenness. My marriage ended in divorce. Work was unstable from the pandemic. The pressure of a failed marriage and a failed business weighed me down. I felt like a total failure, and survival was a daily battleground. In my distress, I sent out countless warning signals to those who would listen.

"I just don't know if I can keep climbing this mountain! If I can't save myself, how can I possibly save my family?" My life was broken and shattered.

I tearfully pleaded to those closest to me, "I fear I will walk with an emotional limp for the rest of my life. I am emotionally crippled and in a wheelchair."

My sister, Elaine, and my daughter Rachel carried me through the darkest of days. A few close friends made a genuine effort to check in and offer support. But, in reality, most people in my life had no idea how far down into a hole I had sunk. I was tired and had no fight left inside me.

On multiple occasions, I nearly admitted myself to the local hospital for mental health treatment because I was afraid I would take my own life. Eventually, I found myself utterly broken and lying in bed with a 9mm in my mouth. I desperately wanted to end it all. I couldn't bear the hurt anymore or see a better day ahead. Feeling completely depleted and unable to continue with life, I cancelled my life insurance too. It just didn't seem to matter anymore. As a result, my blood pressure was off the charts, and I was diagnosed with AFib (Atrial Fibrillation). My heart was sick.

My cardiologist wanted to do a procedure on my heart that would cost $70,000. I could not afford to have this procedure, because I did not have health insurance either. My AFib was so severe my doctor ordered a battery of tests. In order for them to actually perform the tests, I had to be calm enough that I was not in AFib for the procedures.

One particular time, I sat at the hospital for an hour while doctors waited and hoped for me to get out of AFib. Eventually, they just sent me home. When I left, my doctor told me I was a walking time bomb for a stroke, and he prescribed three different medications. However, the medicines were over $800 per month. Again, I had no health insurance. My life continued to spiral downward, and I couldn't see any positive end result. Deep inside, I knew the problem with my health was caused by anxiety and continuous trauma. The constant rumination on past events had to stop if I was to get well again.

During this time, I spent even more hours on the phone talking with my sister, Elaine, who by now had been on staff at Saddleback Church for a number of years.

"I'm going to send you some books to read," she said. "I think these may help you understand how the brain works. Your experiences of trauma from growing up and from the stress in life are affecting your health. You need to rewire your brain."

"Ok, Sis. If you really think reading these books will help, I will do it. I just can't keep hurting anymore."

Reading these books, I discovered I had created my own sickness. As I reflected on my daily habits every night for over twenty-eight years, I realized that I rehearsed and relived the trauma in my mind. Night after night, as I tried to close my eyes to sleep, my past failures and wounds haunted me. My brain dwelled on the pain, becoming my new sense of normal. My emotional home was spent looking in the rearview mirror.

Since my ministry began in 1994, I had longed to minister to men about being a godly husband, an *Image-Bearer* to their wives and children. Devastated and broken, I felt disqualified to help others on their journey, even though I had believed I was created for this purpose. I had lost hope. Peace was elusive, and joy had abandoned me. I knew the correct theological answers, but I felt powerless to do anything.

The Power Twins of peace and joy work as a team in our lives, guarding our hearts and minds from the stressors of this world. The reason joy works in partnership with peace is that "the joy of the LORD is your strength" (Nehemiah 8:10 NIV). It helps keep us sustained, balanced, and walking with God. We also know in the presence of the Lord there is fullness of joy. Jesus said He would give us complete joy, and our joy would be full, so let's look to His example.

The religious leaders of His time accused Jesus of being a drunk and a glutton, which is a very odd accusation. The only thing that makes sense to me is, Jesus was fun to be around. I must interject here that Jesus was without sin and never got drunk. So, in my mind, it makes no sense for them to accuse Him of being drunk unless He was hanging out at the local bar and grill. He was fun.

> *The Power Twins of peace and joy work as a team in our lives, guarding our hearts and minds from the stressors of this world.*

He laughed! And sinners loved being around Jesus. The outcasts of society at that time all loved being in His presence.

Why? Because Jesus was full of joy and peace. Let's remember, though, the purpose of joy and peace is not simply for our own pleasure. We have to stay focused on the bigger picture. Peace and joy are the Power Twins who guard our hearts and minds. Without them, we are left wandering and lost.

Jesus never lost sight of why He was here. He said that He did nothing on His own agenda (John 5:30). Jesus always did the things His Father told Him to do. He said the things He heard the Father say and sought God's kingdom, while living in this world in such a way as to seek and save those who were lost. Being aware Jesus was anointed to give good news to the poor, to bind up the brokenhearted, and set free those who were captives, He lived as a physical representation demonstrating how much God truly loves people.

It is important for us to look at the words *poor* and *captive*, so we fully understand what they mean. *Poor* is not just limited to finances and *being captive* does not exclusively mean being imprisoned.

I actually prefer the word *bankrupt* over poor. This can include being spiritually depleted or emotionally consumed. It can also refer to those who have experienced damaged relationships or physical challenges. The good news is, Jesus came for all of us, wherever we are in life, even when we are spiritually, emotionally, relationally, and physically bankrupt.

Do you know anyone who *is* bankrupt or *has been through* bankruptcy? I've been both. I was incredibly blessed and experienced some big successes—such as being the president of three multi-million-dollar organizations and owning my dream house and car. Parallel to this success were some significant relational challenges in my marriage, which began to erode my peace and joy.

Although I was still able to walk around in my daily life sharing God's Word and truth with everyone and telling them how much Jesus loved them, my mind was fixated on my own pain and internal struggles. Then in 2008, the housing market collapsed, and my business failed. I lost everything I owned and was forced to file for bankruptcy. It devastated me, humiliated me, and crushed me with insecurity as I clawed my way out of the disaster, just to keep my family fed and safe.

Being the father of three daughters whom I loved more than anything on this earth, I did everything in my power to remain a good dad and a strong example for them, despite my pain. My joy and peace were gone. I was bankrupt in every sense of the word. I was angry, wounded, and struggling. Then my heart began to get sick. I was able to keep the external life looking good, but my daily life choices reflected the reality of what was inside me. I did not recognize myself. In retrospect, if I would have taken my own life, the people in my small town would have been shocked.

Outwardly, I looked happy. I was really good at projecting everything was alright. By this point, I had started my own business again, so it appeared as though I was doing well in life. In reality, my heart was sick and filled with cancer because it was void of peace and joy. The Power Twins had abandoned me. God's peace and Jesus's joy were gone, and my heart hurt in every sense of the word.

My turning point was at a funeral of a great man of God, who was the leader of a men's group I had regularly attended. After several weeks of participating in this small group, Jeff and I became very close. We had a mutually transparent relationship that was incredible. Jeff knew I was a wreck! During the group meetings he gave me a safe place where I could be totally honest with him about the choices I made and the thoughts I had.

Nonetheless, he knew how much I loved God. He encouraged me to share my insights about God's Word, and he believed in the calling on my life. Though I truly felt like a leper and even looked like one, Jeff made me feel clean. Again, it hurt my heart to lose such a good friend and spiritual pillar of strength during the weakest moments of my life.

It was at his funeral in the fall of 2020, I ran into a dear brother named Bob, who was also in our men's group.

"How have you been doing? I mean really doing?" Bob asked.

"Not good at all." I was completely honest with him.

"I get it. I've gotten off course too. It's easy to slip and stumble."

We knew all of the right answers, but we just needed someone to walk with us through the mud. We were both bankrupt in every aspect of the word. This began the journey on our individual paths to healing by supporting each other through the process.

Committed to support each other, we decided to begin each day as accountability partners. We began putting in the spiritual work needed to get us back to a place of healing and sought freedom with earnest. The Power Twins of peace and joy would soon return to my life.

Six weeks after Bob and I began our spiritual exercises together, I met Mindy. Words cannot adequately express how incredible and powerful our relationship became immediately. God breathed life into me through her, like I had never experienced before. About four or five months into our dating relationship, I became aware that I was feeling better.

My heart didn't hurt anymore, both literally and figuratively, and I didn't feel like I was going to have a heart attack at any moment.

When she and I were engaged, my desire to be a good husband and provider led to my decision of getting life insurance again, but my medical records documented the AFib challenges, and I was denied. Nonetheless, I was certain I no longer had AFib. My life and our relationship were so filled with peace and joy that words could not express it. The spiritual connection between Mindy and me was—and still is—completely overwhelming. We support each other in our individual lives, do daily devotions together, and pray with each other throughout the day. This has all worked in tandem to heal my broken heart.

Convinced I no longer had a heart condition, I decided to go to a different cardiologist to inquire if they would reevaluate my health to possibly clear my medical records. I knew my heart was healed. My cardiologist ordered a full panel of tests, which showed no signs of ever having AFib or heart arrhythmia issues at all. He updated my medical records, and I was able to qualify for life insurance.

According to the medical industry, AFib is a life-long condition, with no real expectancy of returning to normal conditions. Even the heart surgery that is recommended is not guaranteed. So, what I experienced is a tangible medical miracle. Just to clarify, in the New Testament, there are two different words for healing. One type is an instantaneous healing, *iaomai*, in which a person is healed in such a way that there is no medical or scientific explanation for the change. This is the type of healing Jesus used during His ministry. The other word for healing is *therapeuo*, which is the type of healing that occurs over time, from the inside out. This is where the English word *therapy* is derived.

Through *therapeuo*, healing over time, my hope was restored. Proverbs 13:12 tells us, "Hope deferred makes the heart sick, but when the desire comes, it is a tree of life." When we talk about peace and joy, we must guard our hearts by diligently protecting the things we think, say, hear, or see. It is not just spiritual verbiage; it is as real and important as our need to breathe and has a powerful impact on our daily lives. Clearly, there is a dynamic connection between our spiritual life, physical life, and emotional life. As much as we try to compartmentalize the three areas, they are just as intricately wound together as the Triune Godhead.

Being delivered of my heart sickness is why I have a passion for speaking to men. I don't ever want you to reach the lowest point in your life where you feel helpless, hopeless, and out of control, like I did. Be strong and courageous. Step out in faith. Ask your Father in heaven to help you on your journey as you spend time in prayer and reading His Word. Seek other men to walk with you on this road. Find one or two guys whom you can trust and with whom you can be vulnerable, then be fully transparent with one another about the current status of your lives. Agree to be accountable to one another and allow them to walk alongside you as you work your way back to health and wholeness again.

We need each other to get through this, men! Together, you will find the close companions of peace and joy, and they will fill your heart and home, again.

CHAPTER 8

MODELING HEALING

You might wonder, how did this healing and wholeness happen? *Jehovah Rophe* showed Himself to me through two men. As I mentioned earlier, I ran into Bob at the funeral of a mutual friend. After the funeral, I went home and sat on the balcony. Staring into the night sky, I cried out, "Is it all worth it?"

My dear friend Jeff, an amazing husband and father, was dead. Confused by the sudden loss of a friend, I analyzed my life, which by now was a complete wreck. While still in a critical state of mind and wanting to end everything, I said out loud probably four or five times, "Is it all worth it? Does it even matter?"

While I reflected on the decades of attempting to serve God with my whole heart, I thought about how I'd tried to be the best husband possible and show the *Father-Heart* of God to my daughters. My cell phone rang. It was Rodney, a dear friend whom I had worked with nearly fifteen years earlier.

Before this call, I had not talked to him in at least a year and a half. I answered the phone. "Jim, I felt like God wanted me to call you and tell you, that *you matter.*" He said so simply.

Needless to say, I was stunned. Tears poured down my face as I was completely overwhelmed by God's love for me. The fact that I was saying out loud, "Does it even matter," when at the same moment Rodney called to say, "You matter," was such a supernatural miracle. I truly felt the power and presence of God in my life. I knew Jehovah Rophe was aware of my current situation.

That phone conversation touched me deeply and gave me the courage to reach out to Bob, who agreed to be my accountability partner, study the Word, and pray together with me daily at 5:00 a.m. Both of these men answered God's call in their lives to reach out to me at this particular time. I needed to know I was valued and important, and my life was still worth living.

Jehovah Rophe means *The Lord is my Healer*. God chose to show up through Rodney and Bob. Rodney took a leap of faith and called me to say what he felt like God wanted to tell me, regardless of how crazy it sounded. He had no idea where I was in life at this time, yet he stepped out and made the call that showed *God the Healer* to me. Similarly, Bob chose to take the stripes and get up early every day to do prayer and devotions with me. He walked alongside me on my journey toward healing and wholeness. My healing cost both men something. They both were willing to sacrifice themselves for a friend.

What are you willing to sacrifice? What stripes are you willing to bear for those you love so they can be healed? Are you willing to put their needs above your needs? Are you ready to have a horrible day at work, then come home and throw yourself into the joy of your children's day? Or cook dinner and do the dishes for your wife in order to give her rest and healing for the night? Demonstrating Jehovah Rophe to my family and those around me is just as much natural as it is supernatural.

The Model Employee and Business Owner

Speaking of natural, Jesus was not only the Son of God, but also the Son of Man. He was a regular guy, a dude, one of us. He was a tradesman and worked with His hands as a laborer. Based upon Matthew 13:55 and Mark 6:3, the Greek word for such a tradesman is *tekton*. Therefore, it is most likely Jesus was not only a carpenter but also a stone-mason and metal worker. He worked in the family business. His father, Joseph, was probably well known in the area. Jesus would have traditionally begun as an apprentice when He was young, then later became an employee of sorts, reporting to His dad.

What type of employee was He? Allow yourself to look at this objectively as a man. We know Jesus was without sin, so what does that mean? It means He was teachable. He always told the truth, even when it was difficult. When He measured something incorrectly or made a mistake in a design, Jesus had integrity.

This meant He never went to market with a faulty product. He would have never cut corners for the sake of profit. Is it possible He stressed this point to His younger brother, James, as they were growing up? And is that possibly why James is the one who penned, "To him who knows to do good and does not do it, to him it is sin" (James 4:17)? It is just as important to seek doing good as it is to avoid doing evil.

Jesus encountered difficult things at work too. Let your imagination run wild with this scenario. It is powerful when you reflect on it. He was tempted in all points like we are, which means work was sometimes hard. Customers were difficult to deal with at times. I am sure there were supply challenges and other stress points at work too. Yet, He was without sin.

Jesus also felt the same pressure of provision because He built things for money. Many historians believe Joseph died before Jesus began His ministry, which meant He probably would have had the responsibility of providing for His mother and siblings. As we well know, that is another challenge and difficulty. My point is, as men, we are called to be *Image-Bearers* in every area of life. Still, I want to be clear. This is not a pursuit of perfectionism. It is a pursuit of the presence of God being manifested everywhere we go because He is in us and within us.

Whether we like to admit it or not, our lives are on display. People are watching and listening. As a business owner, I look for teachable people who will fit our culture by interacting well with others. Do our daily choices align with the things we say we believe? Are there character traits we consciously and intentionally model in front of our employees and coworkers? "Do as I say, not as I do," in my opinion, is one of the worst leadership statements ever made.

> "Do as I say, not as I do," in my opinion, is one of the worst leadership statements ever made.

Jesus doubled down against this concept, so much so that He said, "If I do not do the works of My Father, do not believe Me; but if I do, though you do not believe Me, believe the works, that you may know and believe that the

Father is in Me, and I in Him" (John 10:37–38). His life is an example of the truthfulness of His words. We need to be able to make the same statement. The life we are called to live as role models requires us to follow in the footprints of Jesus Christ of Nazareth.

Fun and Full of Life

We've all heard it said, "Work hard, play hard." I believe Jesus did work hard, but I also believe He had a lot of fun and was the life of the party. Almost everyone is familiar with His first miracle, where He turned water into wine at the wedding reception. And yes, wedding receptions, especially Jewish ones, are quite the party. It was obvious Jesus was responsible for this epic night. I don't believe this was just a one-time event, and I'm sure He celebrated and had fun with His family and friends daily. Jesus had fun being around people, and people enjoyed being around Him. Since we know that Jesus was fully human and fully God, He would have experienced the same feelings and emotions we do, including humor. When was the last time you laughed? Laughter is important. Solomon even referred to it as medicine to our bones (Proverbs 17:22).

As we are *Image-Bearers*, people should love being in our presence as well. Everywhere we go—on the jobsite, to the mall, the gas station, or a football game—the tangible presence of Jesus should go with us. It should be present *in* us.

The fact you are reading this book tells me you are spiritually hungry. Therefore, what natural character traits do you want to see manifested in your children's lives? Do you believe education is important? How about integrity or work ethic? Honesty and loyalty? The greatest way to insure these are found in your children's lives is for them to witness them in your life consistently.

I've had men tell me they push their children to get an education because they did not get a degree and have suffered for it. They ask, "How can I demonstrate the importance of education to them? I am too old to go back to school, and I work so much that I don't have time."

My response is simple. You can still be a learner by reading books and improving as a person. This will be your way of demonstrating the importance of education in a real and tangible way. If you spend the majority of your free moments playing golf, working out, watching football, or hanging out at the local sports pub, then your words will ring hollow. Your comments will have a very slim chance of being taken seriously because few people respond well to "Do as I say, not as I do."

Exemplify the model you want your children to become because being a role model requires conscious determination and sacrifice. Jesus was our perfect role model. Therefore, we should live our lives walking in His footsteps. That's what it means when Jesus said, "Anyone who has seen me has seen the Father" (John 14:9 NIV).

CHAPTER 9

A—AFFIRMATION

I n 1997, I felt compelled to leave the youth ministry. I loved serving in children's and youth ministry but felt pulled in a different direction. During this time, I studied and taught the concepts of modeling, affirmation, and discipline. When I left paid ministry, I became a cable installer, commonly known as the cable guy. This work provided new opportunities to meet all kinds of people, since I was in ten to fifteen homes daily.

People from all corners of the world live in Central Florida. It became crystal clear we are all the same. We all fight the same battles and have the same desires. During this season of my life, I had several Bible verses that became bedrock scriptures. Scriptures like:

- "For as he thinks in his heart, so is he." (Proverbs 23:7)
- "For out of the abundance of the heart his mouth speaks." (Luke 6:45)

- "Above all else, guard your heart, for everything you do flows from it." (Proverbs 4:23 NIV)

This study about the words we use made me keenly aware of the direct connection between the words I spoke, compared to the reality of what was in my heart. Because I was not raised in the church and grew up in a violently abusive home, the foundation for what was morally right or wrong was nonexistent. I had no moral compass to guide me, and the needle of my life was spinning out of control. The lack of a *True North* in my life led me down the road of promiscuity. Looking back, I realized I sought affirmation from others during my teen and young adult years to fill the void in my heart. This emptiness later required me to rework my mind and learn biblical truths to repair the damage.

As I went from home to home as a cable installer, I would hear the words men spoke toward their family, and it broke my heart. Sometimes, there was a lack of words spoken, which was equally damaging. I recognized that the men in those homes, just like me, had no concept of the power of words.

Another verse that became part of my mantra of scriptures was Proverbs 18:21, "Death and life are in the power of the tongue, and those who love it will eat its fruit." This is not just some cute little Bible verse we say whenever it is convenient. It is *reality*. When God said the words, "Let there be light" (Genesis 1:3), it happened.

Jesus told us when we speak to the mountain to be moved, it shall be moved (Matthew 17:20). Paul also said in Romans 10:9 (HCSB), "If you confess with your mouth, 'Jesus is Lord,' and believe in your heart God raised him from the dead, you will be saved." Our words carry incredible power.

A year prior to this time, while still serving as the full-time youth pastor, I attended a large event for the athletes at a local high school in Tampa. The guest speaker had been a star player in the late 1970s and shared his story with the teens. He was such a remarkable football player, that he earned a full scholarship to Florida State University.

As a young boy in school, he was diagnosed with a learning disability and required special classes to meet his individual needs. In those days, special classes were visible in the school building. The students who attended them were labeled and identified, which often resulted in public harassment by much of the student body. When he went to college, he took the label and identity of having a learning disability with him.

When new athletes arrived in the fall, the freshmen were usually put on the scout team. Because this young man was such an outstanding player, he was on the varsity team and also had a significant amount of playing time. Unfortunately, he was not as successful in the classroom. Because of poor grades, this talented freshman was expelled from college. Upon his return home to Tampa, he gave his life to Jesus in a very real and profound way. One day while reading the Bible, he read the words of the apostle Paul in 1 Corinthians 2:16 that said, "We have the mind of Christ." This young man took those words literally and believed them with his whole heart to be true for himself.

After his encounter with Jesus, he reached out to his college coach and asked for another chance to get his education and play football again. When this new Christian read the words of Paul, he believed he no longer had a learning disability because he was made new. He believed he had the mind of Christ.

Because this athlete believed he had the academic ability, he worked harder in the classroom and sought help from his professors. Since he saw himself differently, his behavior changed. This change in behavior led to a change of outcome. Later, this incredible young man became an Academic All-American at FSU. The truth is, the only thing that changed was what he believed about himself.

Just to clarify, I am not diminishing the reality of learning disabilities or cognitive impairments that require additional supports or specialized instruction in order for some students to be academically successful. For some individuals, it is an essential part of their educational journey, which can still lead to a successful career path as adults. The difference is, this man's story shows us the belief system he had to overcome was developed and nurtured by the words he heard about himself.

As you go down this journey, look at the power of the words spoken into your life throughout the years. Look to your own belief system as well. Analyze how it developed. Determine if it is based on a truth or a lie. What type of belief systems are you shaping and developing with the words you speak into others?

Are you speaking words of life or words of death into your wife and children? Words carry with them the power of life and death. They can make a person empowered, strong, and self-confident, or they can be destructive and tear down a person's self-worth. Choose your words carefully and speak words of life.

> *What type of belief systems are you shaping and developing with the words you speak into others?*

"Kind words are like honey—sweet to the soul and healthy for the body" (Proverbs 16:24 NLT).

As a Man Thinks, So Is He

Affirmation is "the act of confirming something to be true," according to yourdictionary.com. The reality is, we are always affirming something. The question though is, which testimony or story are we confirming to be true? God has a testimony—His story and His Word. In the chapter on modeling, we addressed the behavior. Now we must ask ourselves if our words agree with His testimony, or do our words agree with the testimony of this world, which has the Father of Lies as its ruler?

In our quest to be an *Image-Bearer*, we must give our words the same weight as we give our actions. Jesus is our model, and the Holy Spirit is our affirmer. In John 16:13, Jesus referred to The Holy Spirit as "The Spirit of truth." Jesus also told us the Holy Spirit will teach us all things (John 14:26). In the same way we represent Jesus as our model, we also represent the Holy Spirit as our affirmer. Jesus not only referenced His life actions but also the importance of His words.

When John the Baptist was imprisoned and about to be beheaded, he sent some of his followers to Jesus to inquire if He really was the Messiah. Jesus's response was remarkable. He spoke about John's position in God. Jesus said, "Assuredly, I say to you, among those born of women there has not risen one greater than John the Baptist; but he who is least in the kingdom of heaven is greater than he" (Matthew 11:11).

Jesus did not verbalize John's current position or practice in life. While John was huddled in prison, struggling with his fear and riddled with doubt, he began to wonder, "Is Jesus *really* the Son of God?"

Jesus could have sent a message of rebuke back, saying, "Really, Dude? You heard God speak. You saw the dove from heaven. Why on earth are you doubting Me now?" But He didn't retort in that way. Jesus declared who God saw John to be. He told John's disciples to go back and tell him to reflect on what he had seen and heard—the deaf, blind, and lame were healed, the dead were raised, and the gospel was preached.

Jesus reminded John of all the things that were putting incredible weight and power not only in Jesus's actions but also in His words. Jesus was affirming the truth to John.

We see this throughout scripture. God renamed Abram, Abraham, which means "father of many nations" (Genesis 17:5), and Sarai became Sarah. God's perspective is reality, even if it doesn't appear to be reality yet. When God renamed Abraham *after* the birth of Ishmael, but *prior* to the birth of Isaac, it showed God's perspective of Abraham and his family lineage.

Even though Abraham had no lineage, God spoke of a family line that was not in existence yet, as though they were. Romans 4:17 (NLT) states, "That is what the Scriptures mean when God told him, 'I have made you the father of many nations.' This happened because Abraham believed in the God who brings the dead back to life and who creates new things out of nothing." The spiritual growth and transformation from Abram to Abraham is profound. God's will is to conform us to the image of Jesus.

We should pursue and desire a similar transition in our lives, from the old man to the new man. There's a popular saying, "We learn from either mentors or mistakes." Let's look at Abram's mistakes so we can learn. Abram had a similar failure as Adam had. He surrendered the responsibility of leadership.

Sarai formulated the plan to be with Hagar. Abram acqui-esced. Wrong choice. The responsibility sat squarely on the shoulders of Abram.

But there was also a distinct difference between their fail-ures. Adam's failure was a direct rejection of God's Word. While Abram's desire was to help God fulfill His Word, his failure had good intentions. He knew God had given him a promise for a son, something for which he had longed and waited many years, but nothing had happened.

So, he decided to take matters into his own hands. The consequences of this failure have reverberated for many gener-ations throughout history. This was an epic failure on Abram's part. Despite such a monumental failure, God still had plans for him, and gave him a new name. By giving Abraham the new name, God spoke words of hope and life into him. It was a promise for a family, one for which he and Sarah had hoped.

Abraham's and Sarah's new names represented the life God called them to live. Abraham would be the father of so many children, we essentially wouldn't be able to count them all, because they would be greater than the number of stars in the sky. God spoke words of life to Abraham and Sarah when He changed their names, and forever changed the tra-jectory of their lives. Are you John the Baptist, huddled in prison, or Abram, longing for a family? Despite any failures in your life, God still has a plan for you and wants to give you a new name too.

We must remember this was not some magic formula that God gave so we could run around thinking we could create our own reality by just speaking it enough times. In the old days, we called that "name it and claim it Christianity." This is an honest assessment of our own lives. We must ask ourselves:

Which testimony do my words affirm? The testimony of what God's Word says about me, my wife, and my children? Or, what Satan, modern culture, and the world system say about me, my wife, and my children?

What we learned from the story about the college athlete is the power of what we believe about ourselves. There are countless books written on the topic of identity and the heart of man. It is safe to say, the consensus among professionals in the psychology world is that all behavior flows from the inside out. What we believe in our innermost being drives the things we do. Therefore, we must sever ties with the words we speak that do not build up our families or those around us.

CHAPTER 10

FALSE IDENTITIES

My belief is that God fashioned all of us to desire approval and acceptance from others. There is nothing wrong with our God-given desire for these feelings, as long as we are living within God's design for people. Looking back on my own life, I am able to recognize where these roots first took hold for me—from the seeds of finding my own self-worth through achievement, success, or sexual fulfillment. Ultimately, God desires for us to feel loved and accepted by Him, which keeps everything in order, so we don't thirst for accolades from those around us.

This is a tricky topic to discuss because we live in a merit-based society. Over the years, my best performing employees were also the most highly compensated. In our human world, those who achieve at a high level and are successful tend to gain approval from others. Let me clarify by stating this is a complex topic. I am not lifting myself up as a self-proclaimed expert, nor am I an educated therapist. I am a man who loves

God, seeks, and believes Him with all I have. Through my journey, I have found truth and peace on this subject, and I simply want to share my testimony and perspective.

My childhood home had little expression of love or acceptance. Early on, I learned I could acquire affirmations from those around me through achievement in various areas. As a child, I was heavily involved in Little League sports, and I quickly learned I could gain approval from successes on the field. Therefore, in order for me to get the accolades I longed for, I had to perform well during the games.

In retrospect, the belief system I developed about myself was, when I performed on a higher level, whether it was at sports, school, the gym, or work, I received the approval I needed from others. People praised me and looked up to me. The approval made me feel important and special. I felt valuable and loved, and I liked it. Those feelings were foreign to me when I was a child, but I found myself gravitating toward approval from others because I learned how to extract their praise through achievement. As a result, I developed a subconscious, mathematical equation in my head:

Achievement/Success + Approval from People = Paradise

It was absolutely euphoric, but little did I know how far off course this faulty belief system would lead me. For the sake of clarity, let's call that inner feeling *my identity*. The Bible refers to this place inside of me as the heart, my innermost being. The power and desire to feel content inside cannot be overstated. In hindsight, it is remarkable how much I continued to up the ante. I did whatever it took to succeed and find approval, even at my own peril. What is driving you? What is the inner pull that drags you through everyday decisions?

Let's continue on with the concept of identity. As men, we are all well aware of and understand the context of the phrase "daddy issues." It is when a broken woman is trying to fill a void that her father created through destructive choices. The sad thing is, everyone around her can see it, but she is blind to the issue; or if she is aware, the inner thirst is so strong, it ends up ruling her life, and she is just along for the ride. This is why it is so important to be aware of our words. Our children need words of affirmation from us so they can grow up to be completely fulfilled by us, as their dad.

The bottom line is, we all have issues. I challenge you to take a moment. Turn off all the noise. Separate yourself from the pressures at work, from family, or worries of the world, and ask yourself these questions: What drives your decision-making? Why do you do the things that you do? Identify for yourself those things that make you want to achieve more of the accolades you desire most in life.

> *Our children need words of affirmation from us so they can grow up to be completely fulfilled by us, as their dad.*

Why did Adam and Eve eat of the fruit from the forbidden tree? Remember, it was the Tree of the *Knowledge* of Good and Evil. Motive matters. As I reflect on my life, I recognize that choices that looked good were made for the wrong reasons. The thirst for approval had way too much influence in the decisions I made. Our life journey leaves a big footprint. Yes, it is about us. Our spiritual and emotional health are important, and we need to be whole and free through Jesus Christ. I believe it is equally important to recognize how our lives affect others. Especially those we love.

To make an analogy, apple trees produce apples, which in turn produce more apple trees. It is called reproduction for a reason. We reproduce who and what we are. So here is my question to you. What are you reproducing for generations to come? Your children's children are affected by your seed.

There are a multitude of internal drivers, or identities, that influence our lives. The four most common types of false identities I have confronted—not only in myself but also in the people I've interacted with over the years—are:

Approval Syndrome
Success-Driven Syndrome
Martyr Syndrome
Unworthy Syndrome

Therefore, if I love my children and want to put their lives on a better trajectory than my own, I must pursue a healthy identity for myself.

Pursuing a healthy identity is not a destination; it is a journey. A process. I am simply challenging you to enter the process. In the book of Hosea, God states, "My people are destroyed for lack of knowledge" (Hosea 4:6).

Men, this is going to take work. It is essential for us to identify which of the Four False Identities we struggle with in our daily lives. After we recognize the source of our struggles, then we can ask God to help us on the journey of replacing our False Identity with our Identity in Christ. This is not an easy process, and when Jesus does heart surgery on us, much like physical heart surgery, it hurts, but the end result leads to health and wholeness.

CHAPTER 11

IDENTITIES OF DESIRE

Approval Syndrome

At the beginning of my third-grade year, I remember taking a standardized test. When the results were sent home, I sat in the kitchen with my parents as they reviewed my scores. I had performed extremely well, so much so that I was invited to go to a gifted children's program at the University of South Florida (USF) two days a week. I remember how incredibly proud they were of me.

Prior to this, I really have no memory of much personal interaction with either of them, other than the extreme spankings I would receive from my father, contrasted with the overly zealous approval from my Little League games. In my mother's defense, she was just trying to survive on a daily basis while raising five children and working full-time. Consequently, their reaction of being proud of anything I had done was foreign to me, and quite frankly, it felt good.

On Tuesdays and Thursdays my dad would drive me to USF. Since he was a mechanic, we rode in his work vehicle. One day, as I got out of his wrecker, I became aware my dad felt uncomfortable with his surroundings. It was obvious he did not fit the environment or culture of a university campus. I remember being very cognizant of the embarrassment he felt and continued to feel each time we went to the university.

This was a remarkable time in my life. I was in the program for nearly a year. I experienced feelings and emotions I had never felt before. My memories included walking into buildings with adults and going up and down the stairs with college students, although I was only a third-grader. The teacher of the gifted program was incredibly kind and encouraging. She made me feel valued and important. I finally felt special, like I mattered. I thrived in this environment.

My regular elementary school system did not know how to deal with a kid like me. So, on the days I went to my regular third-grade class, I was bored. Unfortunately, boredom got me into trouble. Lots of trouble. Things finally came to a head when my elementary school sent a scathing letter home to my parents, which precipitated an abusive spanking. Unfortunately, it was commonplace in our home. However, this one was different.

My dad used a leather belt when he spanked us. He would unbuckle it, and rip it off in dramatic fashion, usually out of extreme anger. He then beat me so violently it broke the belt into two pieces. The irony, in retrospect, wasn't the *physical* pain that was so hurtful. It was the feeling of rejection, total disappointment, and disgust with who I was as a person. That year set the course of my life toward seeking approval in order to feel good about myself and avoid rejection, at all costs. Thus, began my identity of the Approval Syndrome.

Has the feeling of rejection or disapproval created a chasm in your heart that you have tried to fill with the approval of people? It is possible the apostle Paul wrestled with these very issues. He was the shining star as Saul of Tarsus, and the Pharisaical future of Israel was on his shoulders. Because of the change of society in our culture, we cannot even relate to the radical shift from Saul to the apostle Paul.

He became the scourge of society in Jewish culture. Is it possible this is why the Holy Spirit wrote through him in his letters about the constant tension of seeking the approval of man, and resting in the approval of God? Paul was quite emphatic in making this point. At the end of the day, our approval is in God alone, which is what matters most.

Fear of rejection and seeking approval are two sides to the same coin. They feed one another. For me, the fear of rejection became an even bigger driving force than seeking approval. Those lies run deep. The only way to defeat a lie is to replace it with the truth. Jesus said, "You shall know the truth, and the truth shall make you free" (John 8:32).

Abram believed God and became Abraham. Jacob wrestled with God and became Israel. Saul had an encounter with Jesus and became Paul. My prayer for you is to come face-to-face with Jesus and let Him give you a new name too.

So, what is the truth? Again, let's look to Jesus, the Author and Finisher of our faith. At Jesus's baptism, God the Father spoke and said, "This is My beloved Son, in whom I am well pleased" (Matthew 3:17). How could the Father be pleased with Him already? He had not yet performed a single miracle, preached a single message, or faced the temptations from

Satan. You see, God the Father loved Him simply because He was His son. He identified Jesus and established Him as a Son who was beloved, approved, and accepted, independent of any sort of behavioral success.

As I am a child of God, He does not relate to me based upon my actions. Paul says in Ephesians 2:8–9, we have been saved by grace, through faith, not of works, so that no one can boast. The death, burial, and resurrection of Jesus has put me in a right relationship with God. He loves me and approves of me just because I am His son. Not only has my sin been removed as far as the east is from the west (Psalm 103:12), but God remembers my sin no more (Hebrews 10:17). Therefore, I can enter God's presence with boldness and receive His grace and mercy.

Success-Driven Syndrome

Why is it so difficult for pro athletes to retire? Again, I am not a psychologist, but I want to share several stories that we all know about in order to drive home a point. As a Tampa Bay Buccaneers fan, I was deeply saddened when Tom Brady announced his retirement in 2022, following the loss of their last game in the playoffs. In my mind, I understood why he retired. Tom was forty-four years old, had been to ten Super Bowl games, and won seven of them. He had achieved NFL success. Tom Brady is, without question, the greatest football player to ever live. It's safe to say, football is definitely a young man's sport, and at forty-four years old, he had surpassed all other professional football players by remaining a high-performing player in the game at his age. Interestingly though, his retirement only lasted forty days.

We have seen this same scenario several times from other professional athletes. Brett Favre, Michael Jordan, and Michael Phelps are all examples of this phenomenon too. Is it possible who they are and the success they have achieved have become one entity in their own hearts and minds? I am in no way casting a stone at them. I am simply using their lives as a mirror to look into our lives. Yes, their performances and successes are on a level that most of us will never come close to achieving, but what is at the core of their drive for achievement or success? What about me? How can I apply this to my own life? Is my feeling of self-worth and wholeness based upon my success?

In contrast, there are also examples of athletes who have failed on the grandest of stages and vanished from public view. I believe the Success-Driven Syndrome gets ingrained in us from a very young age. Whenever one of our sons or daughters does something good, it is common for us to say, "Good boy!" or "Good girl!" Conversely, if our child lies to us, we call them *a liar*, instead of stating the fact that *they lied*. You see, with our words, we tend to tie together the person with their actions. We cement them together as one, creating an identity. Consequently, it is critical to analyze the way we speak to others and identify the behavior separately from the individual. That is the mystery of the gospel of Jesus Christ.

In God's sovereignty and awesome power, He separates *who we are* from *what we do*. He relates to us as His children, and nothing can separate us from His love. This is the mystery of the gospel—God identifies with us through the behavior of Jesus, because Jesus lived a perfect life. We are the righteousness of God, in Christ. We are complete in Him. We lack nothing. Therefore, we have true freedom. We have freedom to fail and freedom to succeed, but neither one defines us.

I challenge you to look in the mirror. Why are you pursuing success? Again, this is a challenging topic, because as I mentioned earlier, this is a merit-based society. Unraveling the tentacles of an unhealthy Success-Driven Identity can be tricky. Begin to analyze the motivation for your actions. Allow God to shine His light on your motives and prune your unhealthy driving forces. Drill down to find out why success feels so good and has such a prominent place in your pursuit.

> *In God's sovereignty and awesome power, He separates who we are from what we do.*

In hindsight, a real turning point in my life took place in 1984, after I was cut from the football team and expelled because of poor grades. The reality is, steroids were a common part of college athletics and gym atmospheres during this time. Please hear me out. I am in no way condoning this behavior, rather, just trying to set the context. Needless to say, I was taking steroids. I returned home and walked into my local gym very depressed. I had played football nearly my entire life and had been the team captain for most of those years. Since football was gone, I felt gutted and lost. Football was a huge part of my life, and sadly, my identity was interwoven in it as well.

That day in the gym, I ran into some guys getting ready for a bodybuilding contest. Shortly after, they convinced me to compete. With a new sense of purpose, I took all my focus and passion from the football field and fueled it toward the competition. As previously stated, I entered two bodybuilding contests and performed well. I won the teenage division and placed second in the men's division, which fed my Success-Driven Syndrome.

The success from these contests made my world feel right again and deepened the dependency for success to prove my self-worth. The Success-Driven Syndrome was so strong I was willing to do anything, regardless of risk or consequence, to pursue and protect my new identity as a bodybuilder, but the destructive behavior became progressively worse. Not only from the extreme abuse of steroids, but also from the abuse of my body by pushing the limits of my physical strength.

What drives you to make the choices you make? What pushes you so hard you are willing to pursue and protect your identity at all costs, even if it means hurting yourself or others? Search your soul deeply to find the answer.

There is nothing wrong with pursuing excellence or achieving success, but motivation matters. Our success and achievement should be a by-product of who we are, not the driving force to fill a void deep inside. The bottom line is, there is nothing I can do to add to God's love for me or make my relationship any more complete in Him. I am already enough.

CHAPTER 12

IDENTITIES OF WORTH

Martyr Syndrome

People who have this identity problem are stuck in a circumstance and perceive they have no way out. In my opinion, this particular false identity is wrapped around self-pity. If you told me I would fall prey to this, I would have argued with you vehemently. This reminds me of a conversation I had with one of my spiritual mentors early on in my walk with Jesus.

"Jim, the key to walking with Christ is believing there is no sin you are above committing." When he said that, it resonated with me, and I agreed with the concept whole-heartedly. However, life happened.

The details are not important, but over the next twenty years, there was a series of significant events that caused deep pain and feelings of rejection. I suffered great losses. The tragic loss of my business and the financial consequences from it gutted me. To add further injury, some very close relationships were damaged beyond repair. The reality was that very bad things happened to me and I was broken as a consequence.

I replayed the tragedies in my mind's eye. I felt sorry for myself and wanted others to have pity for me too. My wounds became all I thought about on a daily basis. The things that were outside of my control led me to develop a victim mentality. Internally, I had created the narrative that I was giving up my life for the cause of trying to hold my family together. I didn't see at the time that I was focused on control more than on surrender to the Lord. In my mind's eye, *I was a martyr.* I desperately needed God's perspective to move me from self-pity to His perspective.

Unfortunately, through this season of life, I got completely off course in my spiritual walk. Horrible things done to me gradually became my permission slip to act in ways that violated the very things I said I believed. I ended up becoming someone I didn't recognize. Sadly, I drank the fruit punch and believed a lie. I would look in the mirror and ask myself, "What happened to you?" I had no desire for anyone to hold me accountable. I simply wanted them to feel sorry for me. After all, it wasn't my fault I was in this unfortunate state. It was the fault of others, so I thought.

"I am who I am because of the things that have been done to me. I didn't cause all of this to happen, and it's not my fault," I retorted.

Again, I was wrong.

What makes this so remarkable was, I had already been teaching much of what I am talking about here in regard to identity. I knew this stuff inside out, but I just gave up.

Satan is a liar and the Father of Lies. Through the Bible, we are encouraged to make sure we are mindful of his schemes. I literally had swallowed the lie that I was a victim. The truth is, very bad things did happen to me, but I had a choice. We all have choices.

In Joshua 24:15, it says, "Choose for yourselves this day whom you will serve." Deuteronomy 30:19 reminds us we have the choice between life and death, and between blessings and curses. Paul tells us in Galatians 5:16–22, if we walk in the Spirit, then we will not walk in the lust of the flesh. Furthermore, he goes into great detail to specifically name the desires of the flesh, lest we forget. Ephesians 4:22–24 refers to us putting off our former way of life and putting on the new way of life, otherwise known as the old man and the new man.

> *Choose carefully, choose wisely, and choose the path that leads to life.*

The common thread is *choices*. Ultimately, I have to accept full responsibility and accountability for the choices I make on a daily basis. We all have wounds, and we all have triggers, but at the end of the day, we all have the power to choose. Choose carefully, choose wisely, and choose the path that leads to life.

Unworthy Syndrome

Have you ever had a coworker or a friend who always seemed to shoot themselves in the foot? It's not unusual for someone to say about themselves, "I am just not good at relationships," or, "I am not good enough to be a part of that group."

A self-fulfilling prophecy or self-sabotage is a very real thing. Has that been a part of your life? Do you fall prey to the Unworthy Syndrome?

Those who do fall prey, at their core, have a deep-felt belief of unworthiness or shame. This is usually based on past failures and toxic behaviors. They don't feel they deserve to be happy or successful, thereby consciously or subconsciously making choices to sabotage their lives. What I have learned over the years is most people understand the concept of God forgiving them of their sins, but few can genuinely forgive themselves. Their feelings of unworthiness have roots in the failures of their past. They believe that they do not deserve happiness in the future because of the horrible things they have done.

This perpetual cycle of undermining your happiness has at its foundation the false identity known as the Unworthy Syndrome. This is a lie from the pit of hell. Don't buy it, men.

The truth that will set us free from this lie is probably one of the least taught fundamental biblical doctrines in most churches today. It's called the Doctrine of Propitiation. Jesus was our *Wrath Satisfier*. To fully comprehend the magnitude of this, we have to take a step back and look at the totality of the story that makes the cross possible.

God loved you so much that before you ever knew Him or acknowledged Him, He formulated a plan to show you how much He loves you. John 1:1–2 (NIV) says, "In the beginning was the Word, and the Word was with God, and the Word was God. He was in the beginning with God." God placed Himself inside of Mary to be born like a human. He then walked this earth for thirty years as a regular man. He worked with His hands, by the sweat of His brow, to provide for His family. Jesus also felt the same pressures we face today. He was tempted in the same ways we experience, but He lived without sin.

Jesus had a three-year ministry. He walked around villages and preached the gospel. He taught His disciples about God and healed the sick and lame. Jesus experienced rejection and conflict from people. He felt pain and suffering, just like us. He was surrounded by broken, hurting people. Jesus did all that so He could relate to us in every way possible. He was betrayed by those closest to Him and abandoned. Alone.

He was beaten *beyond human recognition*. Sleep-deprived and dehydrated, Jesus was nailed to a cross and died. In doing so, He received the full wrath of God as the complete and total payment for *our* sins. For *your* sins. For *my* sins. For *all* sins. That's what propitiation means. He satisfied the sentence of punishment and pain due to me and you. Jesus truly became our *Wrath Satisfier*. Therefore, there is no punishment left.

I believe that at the core of feeling unworthy is a recognition of either the bad choices I have made or the bad choices others made that affected my life. I use my unworthiness to punish myself for past wounds or transgressions. If I feel unworthy, I don't truly believe Jesus took all of the penalties for my sins to the cross. It implies that the punishment Jesus took on my behalf was not enough, and I deserve some punishment for my past. It calls into question His words, "It is finished." Therefore, I have not accepted that God makes me worthy through His righteousness. The truth is, Jesus has already done it for me. He *is* my *righteousness*.

The person who continually punishes himself through self-sabotage makes his wound perpetually unfinished. He rejects the *Wrath Satisfier*, Jesus.

Do you believe this lie about yourself? Do you feel unworthy of having a great marriage, a successful career, a family, or being made healthy and whole? What do you feel you are unworthy to receive? Call it a lie, and replace it with the truth. God's truth.

As a believer in Jesus Christ, you are worthy to be blessed. You are worthy of being happy, successful, and whole. I will even take it a step further. God desires to bless you abundantly. Ephesians 3:20 (NIV) tells us He is able to do exceedingly, abundantly "more than all we ask or imagine."

Why then would that be God's desire? It is His desire because all of the punishment for our failures was poured out on Jesus. We have been set free from the penalty of sin, which in turn, frees us to step into a new life and live the abundant life God has for us. In Matthew 10:8, Jesus said, "Freely you have received, freely give." God wants to bless and heal us. He wants to give us wholeness and fill us with peace so we can freely give those blessings to others. As we replace the lies from the enemy with the truth of God's Word and affirmations for us, we can then love others the way God loves us.

> *God wants to give us wholeness and fill us with peace so we can freely give those blessings to others.*

When I served as a youth pastor, I learned this lesson from a tragic event that happened one night at a youth group meeting. Each week at the end of our youth group service, we had a time for prayer at the altar. A teenage boy from a family in our church came forward to pray. He sobbed uncontrollably and trembled in my arms.

"My father never spends any time with me." He cried.

I knew the family quite well. While trying to encourage this young man, I was confused because I knew they spent a lot of time together as a family. It baffled me. Finally, one of the things this young boy said to me opened my eyes to the situation.

"Dad will never go to the driving range with me," he said. This young boy was very athletic and loved golf. He went to the driving range every opportunity he had. During the 1990s, quality time was quite the buzz. Like many other families in the church, this father tried to spend time with his children. In an effort to create quality time, they went to a lot of places together and had several family trips. Unfortunately, these trips revolved around the places his parents enjoyed. The problem was that the parents did not realize they were making their son enter *their* world. All he wanted was for his father to enter *his* world. This story is so tragic because this father was truly trying to do a good thing and be a good parent. He didn't really know how.

I knew this dad quite well. He had little to no interest in anything athletic, which led to a disconnection with his son. This man fully understood and appreciated Jesus's love for him. He was well aware his sins were forgiven as a follower of Christ and how much God loved him. This father and son had very different personalities, hobbies, and interests. Sadly, the tangible expression of God's love did not make it to his son.

I learned from this encounter that for something to be an emotional deposit, it must be made using the currency of the local land. In this case, it had to be in the teenage boy's life. It could have been done simply by going to the driving range to watch his son hit golf balls or even watching the PGA together on TV.

The dad just needed to engage with his son. I am not saying the father should have golfed with him. He could have allowed his son to practice while he observed as a way to engage and interact in his world.

This became one of those pivotal moments in my life as

a youth pastor. Through this sorrowful event, I realized the importance of how parents interacted with their children. As a result, I also made it a point to be intentional with the time I had with my daughters. In order for them to feel loved by me, and as their father, I had to enter their world, in their language, as a way that is received as a deposit of my love for them. That's exactly what Jesus did for us. He entered our world, spoke our language, experienced our joys and sorrows, and walked in our shoes. He set aside His world to enter our world, so we could fully understand the *Father-Heart* of God.

One of the greatest examples of this was a dad trying to connect with his daughter. She was thirteen, which is already a difficult age. He tried to connect with her to make her feel valued and loved. This dad was just an overall typical American male. The event took place when the trilogy of *The Hunger Games* had just been released, and his daughter was an avid reader. One night at dinner, while he talked with his daughter, she mentioned how excited she was about a new book series she wanted to read.

A teenage girl was the heroine in this trilogy, which resonated with her. He recognized his daughter's interest in the subject matter, so he asked her if they could read the books together. She loved the idea. They read each book aloud to each other. He would read a page each day, and his daughter would read a page, until they completed the whole series. It was an event that took their relationship to a whole new level.

What made it so neat was anytime someone would ask why he did it, he gave this response: "God wrapped on flesh and entered my world to show how much He loved me. I am trying to wrap on flesh and enter her world to let her know how much I love her."

I hope this story motivates you to think differently about ways to enter your family's world. Remember, the extraordinary is found in the ordinary, day-to-day events of life.

The next story I want to share breaks my heart. One afternoon, Mindy and I were at the pool. Sitting next to us was a mom with three daughters. I heard the girls talking to their mom.

"When is Dad going to be here?" they asked.

"When he gets off work."

About an hour later, Dad showed up, still in his work clothes, which I totally empathize with and understand, as I had been to many of my own daughters' events in my work uniform. In sharing the rest of this story, I am not judging this man, because I don't have all the facts. However, I am just sharing the story from what I observed when he showed up. He sat next to his wife, and they talked briefly. He said hi to the girls and continued talking to his wife. After a few moments, their conversation ended. He either stared at the sky or was staring at his phone, apparently on social media.

He was physically there, but not mentally or emotionally. He wasn't present. Interestingly, while he looked at his phone, the girls attempted to engage him. They kept trying to get his attention, but he would never engage them. You could almost see the sense of rejection in their body language. When he ignored their requests, their mother went out of her way to overcompensate for his absence, playing with them in the pool. The look of sadness on her face and in her eyes was palpable. Sadly, she, too, had been trying to get his attention. She wanted him to show some interest in her and their family, but he didn't. This went on for about an hour until we finally left to go home.

I cannot say this with strong enough emphasis. It is critical you are present when you are with your wife and children. As I referred to earlier, the apostle Paul talks about putting off the old man and putting on the new man. Let's take this concept further and apply it to us, as men. When we come home, we take off the identity of who we are at work, whether a supervisor, an employee, or a president, and put on the identity of "dad" or "husband." You may then ask, "What about me?" Remember, Jesus said He did not come to be served, but to serve and to give His life as a ransom (Mark 10:45), and He is our role model.

Being present, connected, and intentional about entering the world and the lives of those we love is critical as we walk out being an *Image-Bearer* of God's *Father-Heart*. Taking the time to enter someone's world tells them they are worthy and worth me laying down my life for their sake. It says to them, "Meeting your needs is worth more than meeting my own needs," which means, "You are worthy."

Our actions and words are sending out a message to people. The message is either, "You are worthy," or, "You are unworthy." Affirmation is essential to those we love because our words and actions have the power to build them up and make them feel worthy and loved.

CHAPTER 13

D—DISCIPLINE

The next time you hang out with your friends, watching a football game, playing golf, or in any small-group setting, I dare you to say the word *discipline* out loud. What do you think the responses will be? In the circles I run in, that word is not liked. For many, it conjures up the thought of punishment, maybe even wrath. For others, it may be the thought of an extreme lifestyle that is boring and harsh. The odd thing is that we are called to be disciples, which is supposed to be a good thing. So, why in the world does *discipline* make us recoil so much? After all, *disciple* is the root word for *discipline*.

As we read earlier in the book of Hebrews, for us to feel like legitimate sons, our loving Father will discipline us. The scars we carry from this world have created a negative perspective of this word. I want us to view discipline through the lens of this book. We are called to be models, to lead by example. If our heavenly Father loves us and disciplines us in our daily lives, how then do we respond to it? Are we demonstrating appropriately to those around us how we want them to respond to our correction, teaching, and redirection?

One of my favorite lessons from the New Testament is about the Roman centurion, whose servant was sick and nearing death. Both Matthew and Luke tell the story. The Roman centurion was a gentile, and his servant, whom he loved, was deathly ill. His only request of Jesus was to heal this man. Despite his position of authority, this Roman soldier was an incredibly humble man because he recognized his own sinfulness and unworthiness.

We know this because he told Jesus He was unworthy for Him even to enter his home. He asked Jesus to just speak the word for his servant to be healed. At the end of this passage, Jesus said He had not seen such great faith in all of Israel. Can you imagine Jesus, the Son of God, marveling at your faith?

For years, much of the Christian community taught that Jesus was impressed by the centurion because He requested Jesus to simply speak the word. I see it very differently. I believe the key to the centurion's faith was what he said following. "[Just] say the word, and my servant will be healed" (Luke 7:7). Look closely at the passage. He said, "I *also* am a man placed under authority" (Luke 7:8, emphasis mine).

He then described what it looked like when his soldiers did what he commanded of them. This Roman was highlighting a very clear chain of command. He had a leader to whom he submitted and followers who submitted to him. By using the word *also*, the centurion acknowledged he and Jesus had similar positions of authority. This man recognized the chain of command spiritually that Jesus walked. Jesus was submitted to the Father's authority, just as the centurion submitted to his military leader. In today's vernacular, Jesus would have said to the centurion, "You get it."

This Roman leader, who had significant authority, still understood the power of submission. In my viewpoint, this is what moved Jesus so greatly. What I find interesting is how Jesus tied great faith to the understanding of submission. Healthy, sincere, childlike faith is a trusting faith. The act of submission requires the willfulness to give yourself over to someone or something.

Healthy, correct submission always has love and trust as its bedrock. Submission is not domination, nor is it being conquered. God the Father is not trying to beat us into obedience. He won't dominate us into submission to Him. He wants us to trust His leadership and authority and believe His Word as He leads us along our journey. By doing this, we exemplify great faith. This is why Jesus marveled at the person who walked with a submissive heart and labeled it with someone of great faith, because the two are connected.

This particular Roman centurion lived a life of discipline. Even in our military today, we recognize it as a lifestyle. It requires voluntarily surrendering to a chain of command. Our modern military comprises every ethnic group, personality profile, and gift mix together in one unit. Similarly, in our Christian lives, we also have the opportunity to live a disciplined life in a world of diversity of cultures and belief systems. This requires mindfulness. A life of discipline is a choice that is available to everyone. With an honest self-assessment, would you say you live a life of discipline?

This is one area of my life I wish I would have looked at differently when my children were younger. In retrospect, living an undisciplined life was one of my biggest failures as a father. I let external circumstances determine what I viewed as successful. In the mid-2000s, my life looked good on the outside as a man. To say I was undisciplined with how I spent money was an understatement. I was careless and impulsive, with no thought for tomorrow. I made good money, so it didn't matter whether I showed any self-control with my financial decisions. Financial discipline was nonexistent for me.

Likewise, I was physically in very good shape, as I continued lifting weights. I knew how to coach others to get into great shape and to follow necessary nutrition plans to achieve their goals, but I personally violated all of the principles I taught them. For over twenty years, I would get up around 2:00 a.m. and eat chocolate chip cookies and ice cream. Why did I do this? Because I still had many false beliefs ingrained in my heart. I lived most of my life focused on external outcomes. I would knowingly violate wisdom if my foolish choices appeared to have no consequences. I was blessed with a fast metabolism, so it appeared poor food choices did not affect me.

This pattern of behavior that started in my childhood followed me through adulthood. The same thought process that had me excel in high school, yet fail in college, continued into my adult life. I was gifted with the ability to make a good income. Unfortunately, I was as reckless with my financial decisions as I was with my nutritional choices. Because there appeared to be no negative consequences, I fell into the trap and believed my gifts and talents could triumph over wisdom. What's your giftedness? What area of your life appears to prosper even though you willingly ignore wisdom?

When my life came crashing down, the Holy Spirit took me to the story of Samson. This was a painful lesson to learn. Samson was gifted, despite the fact he was violating the principles he was supposed to live his life by as a Nazarite. Even though he was completely undisciplined in his choices, great things kept happening in his life. Victories, if you will. He relied on his own giftedness. Maybe he even lied to himself that God was all right with his choices because of how he was still using him. Outwardly, everything appeared to be working in his favor. Samson's life was good, but the Philistines were coming.

The end of Samson's life is one of the saddest stories in the Bible. He was chained and imprisoned, and his eyes gouged out. The people God once used him to defeat now had him captured. He cried out to God, asking Him to put His Spirit on him one last time. Samson then pulled the pillars upon himself and killed the Philistines as he gave his own life. We know Samson is in heaven with Jesus because he is listed in the book of Hebrews in the Hall of Faith, but what a tragic, sad story and death.

Looking back at my life, all the externals were good, but I made the same mistake as Samson, which led to my demise. My problem was that life seemed good, but the storm was coming soon. We must remember that Jesus told us a storm *is* coming. No one is escaping the storms of life. What is your foundation? The storm finally came for me and exposed my foundation—my undisciplined life. Tragically, my world collapsed, along with my family.

> *We must remember that Jesus told us a storm* is *coming. No one is escaping the storms of life.*

I want to challenge you to look at your own life, especially those of you for whom it may appear from the outside that all is going well.

- Are you submitted to a structure?
- Do you have principles and disciplines in place in your life for how you spend money?
- Do you care for your body?
- How do you spend time growing as a person?
- Are you an active participant in your local church?

This is serious, because if you don't address it now, you will end up in places you never thought you would be.

When Samson was slaying people by the thousands and killing wild animals, he never thought he would be held captive and in chains by the Philistines. When I was in the darkest hours, ready to take my own life, I told several people close to me that I feared I would die like Samson. If you think I am trying to scare you, I am. It is that real. I never imagined being at such a low point in life in my wildest dreams. Keep in mind, healthy fear can be your best friend. We are supposed to work out our salvation with fear and trembling. Proverbs 9:10 says, "The fear of the LORD is the beginning of wisdom." So, pursue viewing discipline as if you were pursuing wisdom.

Is your lifestyle an example of submission and discipline to those around you? Sometimes we make the mistake of trying to be excellent at only the big things in life. Some may be intentional with how they treat people. Others may focus on controlling their temper, or it might be managing money and tithing. Those are all great intentions, but we must be mindful of the small things in life. Jesus said, "If you are faithful in little things, you will be faithful in large ones" (Luke 16:10 NLT).

I want to give an example that may step on your toes. My middle daughter, Amanda, was about ten years old when we planned a camping trip with my friend and his daughter. At the time, I was president of a fairly large organization, and as usual, the time had gotten away from me (because I was not disciplined). I was running late. The gate to the campground closed at 6:00 p.m., and it was an hour's drive from our home. I picked up Amanda at about 5:10 p.m. When we got out of town on the back roads to the campground with no police officers in sight, I tried to make up a lot of ground. I was traveling about eighty miles per hour, and Amanda was in the back.

"Dad, what's the speed limit?"

Integrity was my spiritual theme in this season of life, and I would not lie to her. Like every good parent, I tried to outsmart her.

"I have not seen a speed limit sign for quite some time." I hoped she would simply let it go, and I could continue on my course at eighty miles per hour.

"Does that matter?" she asked.

I remember that moment like it was yesterday. I was frozen in my seat, no streetlights present, only trees on either side of the road. It was January, and the sky was already growing dark. Her words paralyzed me in my moment of truth. What was I going to do? Was I going to lie to her to justify my position or submit to the governing authorities and the laws of the land?

"Honey, you're right. It doesn't matter, and I need to slow down," I said.

I don't share that story to try to elevate myself as some great, epic father. Instead, I share it because I believe modeling submission and discipline is essential. I have shared this story hundreds of times. Most of the time, people just laugh. There have been a few who have really embraced it. When they do, I look to them and say, "You get it."

- How do you respond to God's discipline?
- Do you fight it? Do you resist it?
- Do you grit your teeth and bear it while continuing on the same path?

I ask these questions because earlier, we said we would reproduce our own seed. Again, as the man of the house, I bear the responsibility of leadership in my home. I must set the example to my children and those I lead, so they know how to respond correctly to discipline in their own lives.

CHAPTER 14

SETTING PARENTAL BOUNDARIES

N ow that we have committed to responding correctly to God's discipline in our own lives, how do we discipline our children? Let's go back to 1994, when my oldest daughter, Rachel, was born. At that time, my memory of discipline and what it represented was not what I wanted to re-enact in my own home. I was a young father and an ordained youth pastor just trying to figure the whole thing out. During the 1990s, there were still strong teachings surrounding *spare the rod, spoil the child*. Even the spirit in which I heard people say it would take me back to some bad memories from my childhood. Before we discuss the next story, I want to clarify the purpose of sharing it with you.

Please read it from a 30,000-foot viewpoint. Look at the big picture of the topic of discipline rather than the actual methodologies being discussed. Let's not get caught up in the weeds of *how* to discipline but rather focus on the *motivation* for the need to provide discipline to our children.

I remembered hearing a testimony about a man who gave me a complete paradigm shift regarding discipline. This man was a devout Christian who had a loving marriage and, by all accounts, a peaceful home. He told a story of how his daughter grew up and married, but her relationship with her husband was characterized by physical abuse. This man was beside himself. He didn't understand it.

It was not how he had raised his daughter. She was never exposed to abuse growing up. He was confused about why she tolerated it and refused to leave her husband. Sadly, she believed this man loved her. The father revealed what he felt the Lord had shown him one morning in prayer. Although he raised his daughter when the first anti-spanking movement became more popular, he believed in the use of spanking as a form of discipline. In an attempt to let his daughter know he loved her, he would spank her for whatever misbehavior warranted it. Then he would hug her and say, "Daddy loves you."

As a result, he believed she developed a subconscious association between pain and love. He said if he'd had it to do over, he would still spank her, provided the action warranted it, then ask her a question.

"Does that hurt?" After her affirmative response, then he would make a reply.

"Whenever you do [the misbehavior], it will bring pain into your life."

He thought that if he would have used this approach, she would have subconsciously associated the negative behaviors from her choice with pain from the spanking instead of with love. Later, he would have let some time lapse and reaffirm his love for her by spending quality time with her, hugging her, and stating he loved her.

To say this was an epiphany is a complete disservice to the radical paradigm shift this gave me regarding the application of discipline to my children. On occasion, I did spank my daughters. I should clarify this to say the spankings were never done out of anger, wrath, or a desire to punish. My goal was to attach a negative consequence to negative choices. It certainly was not abusive in the way I experienced discipline as a child.

My daughters, now adults and parents themselves, had commented they appreciated and respected the approach I used toward discipline when they were young. As they reflect on their childhood, they recall never being afraid. Instead, they recognized their actions warranted the corrective measures I used. My daughters will tell you they never felt scared, and it shaped them into the women and mothers they are today. That is all I can hope for as a father, and I am incredibly thankful my approach was radically different than what was used on me when I was a child.

The purpose of this section is to neither defend nor denounce spanking. What's important to note is the purpose of discipline. Discipline is *not* punishment or wrath. Jesus died for the sins of the world, which includes the sins of my children. Jesus was punished for those sins. So, the purpose of discipline is not to invoke punishment but to teach the painful consequences of unhealthy choices.

I view the phrase *spare the rod and spoil the child* in a different light. Proverbs 13:24 (NIV) states, "Whoever spares the rod hates their children, but the one who loves their children is careful to discipline them." This is probably one of the most misquoted and misinterpreted verses in the Bible. We have to look at this verse in conjunction with Psalm 23, which reminds us His rod comforts us. *If spare the rod, spoil the child* means to beat my child for punishment's sake, then how in the world does Psalm 23:4 bring me comfort? To help us clarify and understand the meaning of this, we must ask the following question: What is a rod?

In biblical times, a shepherd had a staff and a rod as he tended his sheep. The staff was used to pull the sheep close when they would stray. In contrast, the rod was a weapon against other animals attempting to attack the sheep. Therefore, the purpose of the *staff* was for *redirection*, and the purpose of the *rod* was for *protection*.

Now that we understand the purpose of discipline, we can look to God's Word for direction. Hebrews 12:7–8 (NIV) states, "Endure hardship as discipline; God is treating you as his children. For what children are not disciplined by their father? If you are not disciplined—and everyone undergoes discipline—then you are not legitimate, not true sons and daughters at all."

Since I am a visual learner, I love to tell stories to create visual pictures. Imagine a beautiful field of flowing hills and green grass. A flock of sheep are in the field eating peacefully. The sheep are surrounded by a strong fence that provides protection, so they feel safe and unthreatened by the dangers on the other side.

Now let's analyze this image more closely. How we view the fence is essential. It is not meant to punish the sheep by keeping them confined to a defined space. It merely represents healthy discipline and safety. The fence's purpose is to keep the wolves out, so the sheep can freely enjoy eating from the lush fields.

Now imagine this. The same picture with no fence. How are the sheep going to eat the grass now without protection?

They must constantly be aware of their surroundings by look-ing up and keeping a watchful eye for the wolves who may try to attack. Their lives would be filled with fear and void of peace from my perspective. In contrast, the sheep who live within the boundaries of protection can freely walk through the field in peace, enjoying the safety the fence provides for them.

This is a mental picture of the relationship between sheep and their shepherd. When Jesus said, "My sheep know My voice" (John 10:27), He meant it literally and figuratively. We know from actual shepherds that sheep truly know their shep-herd's voice. The shepherd, his presence, and his voice are the boundary for the sheep. They know they must stay close to him and follow his lead to be safe.

A home without boundaries, parameters, or discipline is like sheep who have no shepherd. Similarly, sheep without a shepherd are like children without fathers. I believe the author of Hebrews is trying to get us to understand this point. Our children may have a biological father, but they will feel father-less if we are not redirecting, correcting, teaching, disciplining, and providing boundaries. That may seem like a bold state-ment, but without boundaries, we have no moral compass and cannot find our *True North*.

> *Sheep without a shepherd are like children without fathers.*

Today, countless studies show the consequences of fatherless children, whether literally or figuratively fatherless. I stated earlier about the mother and her daughters at the pool that the children had a father. He was physically present yet was absent simultaneously, making them feel fatherless. We can deduce the following: sparing the rod, and having no consequences, correction, or discipline, spoils and rots the children's hearts from the inside out.

To conclude this section, I want to reflect on my experience of being disciplined as a child. I was raised in a generation in which the way my father disciplined me was common. But it was inexcusable. My concern is that the pendulum has swung so far the other way that we have removed the concept of consequences and exchanged it for permissiveness. Therefore, are we creating a generation of fatherless children? We are still harming our children if we replace an iron fist with velvet gloves regarding discipline. Psychologists will tell you healthy discipline is imperative for children to learn and grow. They need the fence of safety, the staff of correction, and the rod of protection to become fit adult members of society.

It is not my place or intent to persuade you one way or another in how you choose to discipline your child. But I strongly encourage you to have a regular, consistent, healthy structure for discipline in your home. Ecclesiastes 4:12 (NIV) states, "a cord of three strands is not quickly broken." Modeling, affirmation, and discipline is a three-stranded cord. They also represent the Triune Godhead. Jesus is our model, the Holy Spirit is our affirmer, and the Father is our discipliner. For us to accurately represent who God is to those around us, all three need to be evident in our lives as men and as *Image-Bearers* and reflect the true nature of the *Father-Heart* of God. In doing so, we point our children to *True North*.

Designed to Be
the Perfect Wife

CHAPTER 15

THE PERFECT WIFE

"When that day comes," says the LORD, "you will call me 'my husband' instead of 'my master.'"

—Hosea 2:16

We've all heard the saying, "It's *not* about religion; it's about a relationship." Quite often, as Christians, we beat our chests and say, "That's right! Yes, Amen!" I wholeheartedly believe the statement above is true, but I challenge you to consider what it says. What does it really mean? The relationship between God and man was broken as a result of sin. Because of the fracture, we were separated from God and incapable of having a relationship with Him. That is why at the Sermon on the Mount, Jesus said, "But seek first the kingdom of God and His righteousness" (Matthew 6:33). What does it mean to seek His righteousness?

Notice the verse does not say, "Seek righteousness," but rather, "Seek *His* righteousness." I believe many well-intended people have read this verse and have set their course just to do good works. Eventually, over time, they become aware of the futility of living up to the standard of righteousness. This underscores Paul's statement in Romans 3:20 (NIV) when he says, "Therefore no one will be declared righteous in God's sight by the works of the law." He also states in Galatians 5:4 (NIV), "You who are trying to be justified by the law have been alienated from Christ; you have fallen away from grace."

What does it mean to seek God's righteousness? Since Scripture is clear that Jesus is the only one who is righteous and the only one who lived without sin, we must seek Him. The book of John tells us that when we believe in Jesus and accept Him as our Lord and Savior, the Spirit of God enters us through genuine faith. Jesus plainly declares, "Unless you are born again, you cannot see the Kingdom of God" (John 3:3 NLT).

Many of you reading this are well aware of everything I just said. Nonetheless, I contend there is more to the story. We must look deeper into Scripture to find the powerful truth about our relationship with God. Paul says in the book of Ephesians that the purpose of earthly marriage—the relationship between a husband and a wife—is so we can understand the mystery of the relationship between God and mankind. Let me ask you this. When is a marriage consummated or considered to be completed? This is not a trick question. The answer is plain. We are all aware of the original intent of the honeymoon, and no one considers a marriage finally completed until the man enters the wife.

I can almost hear you ask, "How in the world is this supposed to have anything to do with my relationship with God?"

Please do not run off on a rabbit trail and think I am trying to sexualize our relationship with God, because I am not. I believe all Scripture is God-breathed, immutable, and perfect. And if the truth will set us free, we need to find the truth that is parallel between a husband and wife and our relationship with God.

To explain this further, upon my belief in Jesus Christ as my Savior, the Holy Spirit entered me. According to Ephesians 1, it is a deposit that guarantees my inheritance to come, which puts me in a right relationship with God. Therefore, in the same way that an earthly marriage is not consummated until the two become one, our spiritual relationship with God is not consummated until the Spirit of God enters me. This makes me one with God and is a fulfillment of Jesus's prayer found in John 17.

I challenge you to examine your soul more carefully. Look hard into the mirror, and ask yourself, "Have I consummated my relationship with God?"

One of the most frightening passages in Scripture is Matthew 7:21–23, when Jesus says, not everyone who calls Him, "Lord, Lord," will be permitted into the kingdom of heaven. He goes on to say, "Many in that day," not some, not a few, but "many." Many will say all the great things they did for Him.

They will point to all of their churchy actions, yet Jesus said, "And then I will declare to them, 'I never knew you; depart from Me, you who practice lawlessness!'" Notice He did *not* say, "I used to know you." He said, "Never." The word *know* is interesting in Greek because it means "a deep, intimate knowing." I think this is where our Western culture and the English language fail us miserably.

In the English language, I can say I *know* Tom Brady, Tiger Woods, and Michael Jordan. I also *know* my next-door neighbor, the mailman, and our 1,700 friends on Facebook. Heck, I know everybody. Knowing *who* somebody is, is not the same as *knowing* them through a personal relationship.

In Genesis 4:1, we are told Adam *knew* Eve and gave birth to a son. If you are reading this as the simple act of sex, you are missing the point. This is a fulfillment of Matthew 19:5, "A man shall leave his father and mother and be joined to his wife, and the two shall become one flesh." In the same way, the last prayer Jesus prayed before He was arrested was for all of us to *become one* with the Father (John 17:20–23), and Jesus wants us to know God truly.

You are about to answer the single most important question in all eternity: Have you *become one* with God, thereby entering into a marriage with Him? Do you really *know* Him?

The question is vital because the Bible calls us the Bride of Christ, and we must be made one with God through Jesus. Or do you simply agree intellectually with the story and try to live a good life? Men, we live in the times Hosea prophesied about when he said we would call Him "husband" one day (Hosea 2:16 NIV).

> *Have you* become one *with God,* thereby entering into a marriage with *Him?*

Viewing my relationship with Jesus through this prism and paradigm had one of the most profound effects on my entire faith walk. It seemed like just yesterday when I was in a challenging situation at home. My marriage was a real struggle. One day, while in prayer, I thought I was praying for my marriage. In reality, I was actually complaining about my wife. I felt led by the Holy Spirit to go to the book of Hosea and study it. Hosea 2:16 jumped off the pages.

I was asked the question, "What type of wife are you to *Me*?" Going forward, anytime I complained or grumbled to God about what was lacking in my relationship with my wife, I felt like the tables turned on me.

"Are you making *Me* feel that way?" This drove me to attempt to be the wife toward God I was longing for my wife to be toward me.

What kind of wife are you? Are you the wife to God that you want your wife to be to you? If you want or expect things from your wife that you have not given to God, then you are self-deceived and a hypocrite. Have the integrity and pursue being the wife to God that He designed you to be. You will set an example for your wife at home in doing so. After all, God is the designer, and we must honor His design for marriage.

CHAPTER 16

DESIGNED TO BE MONOGAMOUS

he first two commandments made it very clear. We are not to serve, bow down, or worship anything, or anyone, other than God. The Old Testament prophets repeatedly called out Israel's adultery and called them a harlot. The prophet Hosea spoke in very clear language about this subject:

> For they shall eat, but not have enough;
> They shall commit harlotry, but not increase;
> Because they have ceased obeying the LORD.
> Harlotry, wine, and new wine enslave the heart.
> My people ask counsel from their wooden idols,
> And their staff informs them.
> For the spirit of harlotry has caused them to stray,
> And they have played the harlot against their God.
>
> (Hosea 4:10–12)

I'm sure there's a large percentage who read this book who have had to suffer the effects of adultery. In my life journey, I have known many people who have walked that road, and it is one of the deepest wounds of all. Betrayal cuts to the core of the union between a husband and wife. If there are any of you who have committed the act of adultery, this is not an attempt to heap condemnation on you or to rub your face in past sins, but you must repent and seek forgiveness.

If you have entered into marriage with Jesus, His blood has washed you and cleansed you of all unrighteousness. He remembers your sin no more. Jesus also commands us, just as He told the woman caught in adultery, to go and sin no more (John 8:11). That being said, we cannot shrink back from having an honest, probing conversation about this topic.

To be certain that we get everyone on the same page, it is vital for us to revisit the Sermon on the Mount. Jesus said, "But I say to you whoever looks at a woman to lust for her has already committed adultery with her in his heart" (Matthew 5:28). He then continued the passage by stating, "If your right eye causes you to sin, pluck it out and cast it from you. . . . And if your right hand causes you to sin, cut it off and cast it from you; for it is more profitable for you that one of your members perish, than for your whole body to be cast into hell" (Matthew 5:29–30).

Whether you like it or not, this is a lesson about sexual sin. Jesus put everyone on a level playing ground in this passage. Those who commit the act of physical adultery, those who commit sexual sin in their mind, those who commit sexual sin with their right hand, and those who commit sexual sin with their eyes—all of those acts constitute committing adultery, not only physically but spiritually as well.

I believe sexual sin is the modern-day leprosy for men. It is virtually eating men alive, from the inside out. We are literally attempting to have a marriage with God, while being an active adulterer. Adultery is like an atomic bomb. The explosion it causes is catastrophic. I cannot imagine the pain this must cause God. Sadly, I have had the opportunity to talk to people who have walked in on their spouse and caught them in the act of having sex with someone else.

For a person to witness their spouse having sex with another person is emotional Armageddon. No matter how good we have become at hiding our unfaithfulness from others, God, as our husband, is forced to watch our unfaithfulness to Him. This includes pornography of any kind, looking at or thinking lustfully about others, and masturbation.

According to a 2014 research poll conducted by Barna Group, 77 percent of Christian men aged 18 to 30 view pornography once per month, and 77 percent of Christian men aged 31 to 49 "looked at pornography while at work in the past 3 months."[1] It is safe to say that this problem has most likely become significantly worse since this study was conducted. As you can see, men, we have a deadly cancer growing in the body of Christ. Statistically, there is a high probability that over half of the men reading this book are committing sexual sin right in front of God. Men, masturbation is not OK. For years, I lied to myself, trying to keep my thoughts pure, but the reality is, it is still sin. It is outside of God's Word and God's design for masculinity. As we know, the wages for sin is death.

---

[1] Joel Hesch, "2014 Pornography Survey of Christian Men," Christian News Wire, October 7, 2014, http://www.christiannewswire.com/news /3446774899.html.

Paul tells the church of Thessalonica, "For this is the will of God, your sanctification: that you should abstain from sexual immorality; that each of you should know how to possess his own vessel in sanctification and honor, not in passion of lust, like the Gentiles who do not know God" (1 Thessalonians 4:3–5). In my view, there is no greater act of self-provision than sexual sin. Either *God* is Jehovah Jireh, my Provider, or *I* am my Provider. Some of you right now may be feeling completely overwhelmed because you have tried and failed many, many times. Trust me, I understand. More than you know. I want to give you *hope*, and you can be set *free*.

In the same way God asked Adam, "Where are you?" I want to ask you a few questions. What do you believe about pornography and sexual satisfaction outside of God's design? Do you believe it is the really fun, pleasurable stuff you are not supposed to do, or do you believe Paul when he says the wages of sin is death? Pornography and sexual satisfaction are as deadly as drinking poison.

When I was in youth ministry in the 1990s, I shared this next story many times with the teenagers in my group. Many of the high-school kids in my youth group were new drivers and were excited about their ability to drive a car. During this time, Josh McDowell's *True Love Waits* campaign was in full force. It was indeed a national phenomenon among the Christian community. Sexual purity was something we discussed on a regular basis.

When talking to teens, my conversation with them would go something like this.

"When was the last time you had to fill up your car with gasoline?" Their answer was irrelevant, so then I would ask:

"While you were driving to the gas station, did you have a pep talk trying to convince yourself you were not going to drink gas, but instead put it in your car? Did you rebuke the devil, cast him out of your mind, and say, 'I will not put that nozzle in my mouth. Not today, Devil, you are not going to win'?"

By this point, they were looking at me like I was crazy.

"No, of course not," they said.

"Why?" I responded. I usually received a blank stare in return. I asked again, stating it was not a trick question.

"Because it will kill me."

Questioning them again, I asked, "How do you know it will kill you? Have you ever seen someone do it and die?"

They said again, "No, of course not."

We would then discuss the fact it must be something they had to take by faith.

This example reinforces the power of belief. As long as we believe sexual sin is the fun stuff we cannot do, we will never be free. We might abstain from these things, but still not be free. For us to truly be free, we must believe the truth of God's Word. Pornography, sexual sin outside of God's design, and self-provision are like drinking gasoline, because the wages of sin is death. It is toxic. It brings nothing good and leads us on a miserable path of defeat, destruction, and death. Therefore, run away from sexual immorality, because it "is a sin against your own body" (1 Corinthians 6:18 NLT).

Be bold and strong, men. Pull out the sword of the Spirit, which is the Word of God, and fight. Psalm 19:14 says:

Let the words of my mouth and the meditation of
my heart
Be acceptable in Your sight,
O LORD, my strength and my Redeemer.

When the temptation for sexual sin attacks your fleshly desires, fight back, but not with willpower, because you will lose. Instead, speak the Word! It is impossible for you to recite out loud Psalm 19:14 *and* commit sexual sin at the same time.

I don't care how many times you have to repeat it, just do it. There were times in my own journey when I recited this verse a hundred times to resist the temptation, until I either fell asleep or the desire left.

We have a choice to either speak God's Word out loud or surrender to the attack. Choose either life or death, but take heart in this. I stand before you completely liberated and whole, with absolutely no desire for any form of self-provision or sexual sin. God's Word has set me free. He will do the same for you, my friend. He will do the same for you. At the risk of sounding like I am oversimplifying something that could be very complex, I want to challenge you to *turn on the light*. Darkness must flee when light comes on. Allow *God's light* to shine in every area of life. Submit to God, resist the Devil, and he will flee (James 4:7)!

One of the ways to submit to God is to accept full accountability and responsibility for your actions. This was something Adam did not do. He actually blamed Eve, the snake, and God for what happened. Heck, God gave him woman anyway. Was it everyone else's fault, except Adam's? No, it was Adam's failure.

What excuses have you made to justify your choices with sexual sin, or, do you ascribe to Sigmund Freud's secular psychology that proclaims you are who you are because of how you were raised or because of the things done to you by others?

I read Steven Covey's book in 2001, *The 7 Habits of Highly Effective People*. The section about being proactive was life-changing for me. Covey defines being proactive as "taking control of the space of time between stimulus and response."[2] Stimulus is anything that is pushing me, whether it be feelings, thoughts, or emotions I may be experiencing, to act in a certain way. The truth is, there is a space, a moment in time when I am in complete control, between the stimulus and the response, which precedes the behavior that I choose.

There is an incredible article by Viktor Frankl titled *The Last of Human Freedoms*. Viktor states, "Everything can be taken from a man, but one thing: the last of human freedoms to choose one's attitude in any given circumstance, to choose one's own way."[3]

Viktor Frankl was an Austrian neurologist, psychiatrist, philosopher, author, and Holocaust survivor. He was kept in four different concentration camps, one of which was Auschwitz. He suffered severe malnutrition, torture, and emotional abuse. What he learned was that regardless of anything that was done to him, or the circumstances around him, he was in control of his attitude and response. He chose to treat his captors with kindness, grace, and mercy, and he chose to give hope and positive encouragement to his fellow captors. After this experience, Frankl penned the article referenced above.

The key to you being free from sexual sin starts when you accept full responsibility and accountability for the choices you make. The things that were done to you as a child or by former relationships can be the external stimuli, much like the Nazi guards in Viktor's life. But at the end of the day, you and I

---

[2] Stephen R. Covey, *The 7 Habits of Highly Effective People* (New York: Free Press, 2004), 71.

[3] Viktor E. Frankl, *Man's Search for Meaning* (Boston: Beacon, 2006), x.

have a *choice*. We control the space between what happens *to us*, and the actions that come *out of us*. We must own that space. This is the beginning of turning on the light and watching the darkness flee.

Romans 12:2 states that we are transformed by the renewing of our mind. This was also a big part of my journey toward true freedom. One of the books I read on this subject was *Switch on Your Brain* by Dr. Caroline Leaf. She is a tremendous resource to help you rewire your brain, and she has several books on this subject.

Keep the pursuit of renewing your mind in Christ as a driving force so you can be a monogamous wife toward God. You are pursuing faithfulness *to* God, and purity *with* God. That's where the power lies. Darkness will flee as a by-product of the light that shines within you. Pursue God with your whole heart and let His light shine through you.

> *We control the space between what happens to us, and the actions that come out of us.*

CHAPTER 17

DESIGNED TO BE INTIMATE

L et's revisit the garden of Eden and the break in the relationship between man and God. In the original design, Adam and Eve were naked and unashamed. They were unashamed to be fully transparent not only with each other, but also with God. Genesis 3:8 states Adam walked with God in the cool of the day. I wonder what those conversations were like. I would imagine they went on for hours and were void of sin, guilt, or shame. They were filled with deep, meaningful conversations with one another. This was an incredible time period in the history of our world, which was lost along with the garden of Eden.

What I find interesting was after Adam and Eve sinned, they did two things. They attempted to clothe themselves to hide from each other, and they literally hid from God. But He went looking for them. God inquired, "Where are you?" God already knew where they were, but the question was more for Adam to know himself than for God to know.

Did you notice that God initiated the conversation with Adam? Is it possible God missed walking in the cool of the day and having those intimate moments of unbroken fellowship? I venture to say He probably did. It had been pure, but a line was drawn between the two of them after the fall. A line that only Jesus could restore.

I believe Jesus concurs with this point in John 4:23–24, when He says, "The true worshippers will worship the Father in spirit and truth; for the Father is seeking such to worship Him. God is spirit, and those who worship Him must worship in spirit and truth." God is seeking the same level of intimacy from us. He longs for it.

Again, let's look at the example we can all relate to, that is, the natural marriage. Envision the following scenario. You've had a hard day at work and are on your way home. In your mind, you are planning a nice romantic evening with your wife. When you get home, you have dinner with the family and get the kids off to bed.

You hint around to your wife about your agenda, but it is received less than enthusiastically. It hits you like a punch in the stomach, so you try to explain your position and need for intimacy with her. Then you're told something like this.

"OK, it's been a while," or "Let's hurry up because my favorite TV show comes on in twenty minutes." Your heart sinks even deeper.

The point of the illustration is neither to rally other men to feel sorry for you nor to make your wife out to be a poor or pathetic wife. The point is to lead us to these questions: As God's wife (the church), what is your response when God seeks intimacy from you? Do you reject God in the same manner?

"Well, I haven't read my Bible in a while, so I guess I should," or "I haven't really prayed for a while, but I should since it's the right thing to do." Possibly this, "I sure hope the pastor hurries up and finishes this message because the football game comes on at 1:00."

It is humbling to come to the realization we have the ability to make God feel sad and brokenhearted in the same way our wives can make us feel. Also, don't forget, you can make your wife feel this way too. I don't know about you, but that's enough to help me stay focused on the fact that Jesus is my first love.

Let's dig a little deeper. What is your worship experience like in church on Sunday mornings? Are you an active participant? Do you get lost in the moment, as if it is only you and God? This is in no way a judgment, just an observation, but most Sunday mornings in the churches I have attended, many of the men are not participating. They just stand there. God longs for a relationship with us that includes involvement on our part. I am not saying you have to run up and down the aisles or wave your hands over your head like a wild man. My point is, are you engaged? Do you show interest? Do you open your heart, mind, and spirit so you can listen to the Holy Spirit?

If our relationship at home or our relationship with God looks like the scenario of longing for intimacy from our wife, then there is something wrong. Something is *deeply* wrong. We have a love problem. It is impossible for us to fully love God through effort or hard work alone. It only comes through revelation or epiphany.

In 1 John 4:19, we are told that we love God because He first loved us. Romans 5:8 states, "But God demonstrates His own love toward us, in that while we were still sinners, Christ died for us." Paul also writes in Romans 8:39 that nothing can separate us from God's love. When we have a full revelation of God's love for us, as expressed through the sacrificial death, burial, and resurrection of Jesus Christ, we are able to respond with a love that flows from deep inside us. Then and only then can we love others with the same kind of love Jesus has for us.

I'll never forget the first few weeks Mindy and I were dating. We had deep, transparent, honest dialogue for hours. Day, after day, after day. Sad but true, I had never experienced this level of intimacy through deep, meaningful conversation that involved sharing hearts and emotions with another person in my entire life. I

> *When we have a full revelation of God's love for us, we are able to respond with a love that flows from deep inside us.*

remember thinking, "Oh, my God! This is how the relationship between man and woman is supposed to be."

It was as if a cavernous, empty void in my life was finally getting filled for the first time. I knew right away we were going to get married. I also remember having the epiphany other men needed to know and experience this same feeling too.

Men, this is where life is. This is the will of God for your life. Seek it, pray for it, and go to war with anything that tries to block or prevent intimacy with your wife from happening.

When we learn how to walk in God's love for us, we can be naked and unashamed or fully transparent about ourselves. We can have the ability to stand white as snow not only in our relationship with God but also in our relationship with our wife and others.

Let's return to the example of your planned agenda for an evening of intimacy. Allow me to interject a slight twist on the story in the form of a question: Were you planning a night of intimacy, or were you planning a night of sex? There is a difference. It is nearly impossible to have sex with your wife with your clothes on. So, is it possible that you are wearing invisible, emotional clothing in the form of cares from this world, shame, failures, or hidden secrets, which are blocking your ability to be intimate with your wife? Is it blocking intimacy with God too?

God is seeking those who worship Him in spirit and truth. He is calling, "Where are you?" I encourage you to stop hiding. Confess your sins to an accountability partner so you can be healed. Trust the blood of Jesus has cleansed you, and stand before God naked and unashamed. Be fully transparent about who you are, where you are, and what you've done. Your spirit will then cry out in worship and gratitude, praising His name, and you will be set free in Jesus Christ.

CHAPTER 18

DESIGNED TO RULE AND REIGN TOGETHER

O riginally Adam and Eve were designed to rule and reign in the garden of Eden as a team, completing each other. The two became one. One unit, if you will, and this theme continues throughout the New Testament. It states we are colaborers with Christ and that we are seated in the heavenly places with Him. One of Jesus's most famous teachings was when He said, "Come to Me, all you who labor and are heavy laden, and I will give you rest. Take my yoke upon you and learn from Me, for I am gentle and lowly in heart, and you will find rest for your souls. For My yoke is easy and My burden is light" (Matthew 11:28–30).

To fully understand what He is saying, we have to look at the picture Jesus is creating for us. A yoke is an apparatus with two holes in it for oxen to slide their heads into, and it rests across each of their necks so they can walk in unison, pulling the load together. When Jesus said being yoked to Him would give us rest, He was not saying we would just lie there in the yoke while He drags us around with Him.

On the contrary, He communicated to us, "I will come alongside you, walk with you, and help you pull the load." A side note here is that the Greek word for Holy Spirit is *parakletos*, meaning "one who comes alongside." Therefore, we can take comfort in knowing the Holy Spirit walks alongside us as we travel through life's journey.

Our relationship with God is meant to be *interdependent*. Initially, that may sound crazy, but we are not only to be called colaborers with Christ. We are to join with Him in the endeavor. Paul tells us in our ministry of reconciliation that God is appealing to the world through us. We are the hands and feet of Jesus. I would call that an interdependent relationship, in which we work collaboratively yet function autonomously.

Furthermore, I venture to say most people fall either into codependent or independent relationships. How we relate to others is a learned behavior ingrained deeply into our psyche from childhood. Think about the relationships you have with the people in your life. What destructive behavior was normalized in your home during your childhood?

> *What destructive behavior was normalized in your home during your childhood?*

On the one hand, my father was an alcoholic and was intoxicated daily. He was highly volatile and ruled with an iron fist. On the other hand, my mother was one of the hardest working humans I have ever known. Not only did she work a full-time job, but also she managed the home, kept us fed, and stayed up late at night hand-sewing all of our clothes. She did every-thing in her power to keep the family unit moving forward, regardless of the horrific circumstances. This environment was a petri dish for codependency, and I became the poster child for it.

As the youngest in my family, I was completely unaware of the codependency in our home, but as I grew older, I was very social and had a lot of friends. I didn't realize, even then, how much my family life would affect my future relationships with those closest to me.

Finally, when I was at the end of my rope in 2020, I began to put a lot of work into my mental health to rewire my brain. I realized I was the classic adult child of an alcoholic. To help me work through this revelation about myself, I read *Codependent No More* by Melody Beattie, which I recommend. Caution: this book is not for the faint of heart. This book will enlighten you but, at the same time, is incredibly difficult to read. It challenges the reader to reflect on oneself with hon-est introspection. Just as the crucifixion was horrific and ugly, the resurrection was beautiful. This book was my crucifixion in many ways, but my resurrection was on the way.

Having a healthy relationship with your spouse or God is impossible when your foundation rests on codependency. You can either be so needy you suck the life out of your partner because your own needs are insatiable, or you can be so con-trolling in trying to fix everybody that you break everyone. For the codependent person, you become your own worst enemy.

Keep the picture in your mind about the yoke Jesus ref-erenced. We've established that my marriage on earth and my relationship with God should run parallel. That said, ask yourself these questions: Am I yoked with my wife on this life journey? Are we fitted together in the yoke, walking in unison, and pulling as a team?

One of the most common mistakes men make in their marriage is expecting their wife to carry the bulk of pulling the yoke. They expect her to take care of the household duties and tend to the needs of the children. In addition to those things, she stays on top of his schedule and makes sure her husband makes adult decisions. In many ways, I have watched some men turn their wives into their mothers, although they were unaware of it.

In no way is this meant to disparage or attack their character. They don't know the transition has slowly taken place. Often, these men act out as the little boy inside who never felt a healthy, deep love from their mother. In a weird, unhealthy way, they try to heal a painful wound through the relationship with their wife, all the while killing the ability to have healthy intimacy with her. After all, how intimate can you be with your mother? It creates a subconscious disconnect.

Paul said when he became a man, he put away childish things. It's time for us to grow up because:

- boys are impatient
- boys are not kind
- boys want what others have
- boys love to show off and be seen
- boys are proud
- boys seek their own way
- boys are rude
- boys are easily provoked to anger

- boys are always thinking about how to get in trouble
- boys plan dark deeds
- boys do not like the truth
- boys easily give up

When we have matured:

- men can suffer for long periods of time
- men are kind
- men do not want what others have
- men are not attention seeking
- men can humble themselves
- men do not seek their own way
- men are polite
- men are slow to anger
- men control their thoughts
- men do not think on evil things
- men love the truth
- men are willing to endure all things

This is the target as you walk in partnership with your wife. Many of you may have recognized the previous statements loosely came from 1 Corinthians 13, the "love" chapter of the Bible. The *pursuit* is to walk in *love*.

On the other end of the spectrum of codependency is *independency*. The independent mindset does not walk in love and can take various forms. At the core of an independent person is someone who is egocentric: one who is self-centered and focused on his wants and desires.

In today's society, an independent person is often applauded and esteemed. Independency is a respectable quality, as long as it keeps in balance with oneself. It requires an individual to put the needs and desires of another above one's own needs, even while still being independent. Occasionally, it can look good on the outside, but at its core, independency is an obsession with self. The egocentric person's first thought in every situation is how it impacts him, with no regard for those around him.

The independent heart is like cancer to a relationship. Unfortunately, like cancer, it can go undetected for many years. When my youngest daughter, Karissa, was a teenager, we decided to attend a concert. We were not satisfied with merely going to the concert but wanted to be in the front row, center stage. This band was very popular and well-known for interacting with those at the front of the stage, which is referred to as the pit. Those tickets are referred to as general admission tickets and are first-come, first-served. To be on the front row meant we needed to be first in line. Achieving this required us to camp in front of the venue and wait until tickets went on sale. We arrived a few days before the concert, ensuring we would be in the front of the line. We ended up having a great time together, spending the evenings talking to the other teens there. This resulted in extensive conversations about life during the evening gatherings. With great curiosity, they asked me the same question multiple times.

"Why are you here?"

Taking my cue from the father in my illustration in chapter 12, who read the books with his daughter, I said, "I'm trying to enter my daughter's world to show her how much I love her." Their answer made my heart sink.

"My father would never do this with me," one teen remarked. Is it possible these dads refused to go because they were thinking through an independent mindset? Were they being egocentric, putting their discomfort ahead of the positive impact it could have on their child?

This is in no way an attempt to stir up condemnation or look down on anyone as a father. Allow this story to work as an MRI to expose the cancer of an independent heart.

Now let's apply this to your own life. Imagine you have just come home from a long day at work. As you enter your home, your wife appears frustrated. In your thoughts, you secretly hope she will ask you about your day so you can talk about your frustrations or successes. You are aware the kids are home from school, but you want to relax and calm your mind after the hard day you've had at work. You change clothes, sit on the couch, turn on the TV, and search social media on your phone. Your daughter wants your attention, and your son is elusive, but you brush them off to entertain themselves.

Are you egocentric? Are you focused on the highs and lows of your workday, or have you mentally checked out? As men, we can be so task-oriented that we often forget to check in with our family members. We may come home exhausted from the workday, change clothes, and just want to turn on the TV. But are your kids wanting your attention? Perhaps your wife is feeling depleted from her day at work and needs a hug from you to feel secure, or maybe just a listening ear.

Before you go through another routine day in your life:

1. Open your eyes to the people around you.
2. Look through a new lens and see life from that perspective.

3. Be the father or husband who is attentive to his family's needs.

4. Go out of your way to make them feel important, valued, and loved.

It doesn't have to be grandiose. It can be as simple as a word of encouragement, a moment to listen, or a hug. At the end of the day, we are called to lay our lives down for others, and we must rise to the occasion.

The fact you are reading this book tells me you believe you are supposed to be leading your home and/or your marriage as part of your masculine responsibilities. I want to press in defining what a Christ-centered leader looks like versus what the world defines as leadership. Many people think the leader of a business is also the boss. As the leader of our home, our job is not to boss our family members and treat them as subordinates. We are to live as teammates with our wives and as role models for our children.

The Bible says in the same way Christ is the head of the Church, the man is the head of the home and marriage. Therefore, I can falsely deduce again that I am the boss. I passionately believe a leader is not a boss, and a boss is not a leader. Being a leader, by definition, means there are other people with me, and we are going someplace together. As the leader, I show the people where I want them to go. Therefore, it is impossible to be a leader in that context and still be independent.

A boss tells people where to go, what to do, and how to do it. A boss is independent and maintains supreme authority. Totalitarians. "I said it, and that settles it." Bosses may think, "I know what's best, so if everyone does what I ask when I say it, then we will all be happy."

The mindset of a completely independent person is an obsession with self, is egocentric, and is built on a foundation of pride. James 4:6 states, "God resists the proud, but gives grace to the humble." To adjust our way of thinking from boss to leader, we must be willing to accept correction and take accountability for our behaviors.

The next challenge may be difficult for you, but I encourage you to sit down with your wife and give her the freedom to be completely honest with you. Have a pencil and paper ready and ask her these questions:

- Do my words or actions make you feel like you are my mother?
- Why do you feel that way?
- Do my words or actions make you feel like I am your boss?
- What actions or words do I use that make you feel as if I am your boss?

Do not defend or justify her responses. Just listen. This may require you to push her to open up. It is critical for you to go out of your way to let her know she is safe and she can trust you. So, allow her the freedom to get it out. Simply write down what she tells you. Be sure to write down the specific things she says that you contribute to the relationship that cause her to feel the way she does.

Please do not *make a bunch of promises.* Force yourself to look at her emotions and feelings through her perspective or viewpoint. Empathize and relate to her feelings, and *never,* I repeat, *never use these words against her in the future.* Simply commit to working on the issues and being a better representative of Jesus.

I encourage you to start praying regularly together. Ask God to help you, as the leader of the home, to represent Him correctly to your family as you rule and reign together as a team. Through this, you will learn to celebrate the unique gifts you each have and experience the power of submission to each other. As you work in unison with the Holy Spirit, He will firm up the foundation of your marriage. It will bring a feeling of completeness to your union and home that you may have never known.

Please do not undervalue this design aspect of a man's relationship with God and people as you journey down this road. As we are men walking with God, this element of our relationship is as critical as the resurrection was to the crucifixion. *Masculinity by Design* requires us to be strong, spiritual leaders in our homes, represent the *Father-Heart* of God to our children, and love our wives correctly. We must follow in the footsteps of our role model, Jesus.

Though we talk about these items as distinct elements, they all work together to create God's symphony, just like instruments in an orchestra. As the conductor directs the musicians to play their parts as a collective group, their music becomes a beautiful melody when joined together as one. This is our goal—oneness.

Designed to
Be a Disciple

CHAPTER 19

DISCIPLESHIP STARTS N.O.W.

In the summer of 2007, life was good. My marriage was still fractured but functional, and my relationship with my daughters could not have been better. Our electrical and air conditioning company had grown into a thriving organization. We had one hundred twenty-eight employees and forty-four vehicles. There was so much new construction that the entire fleet of vehicles was in the field every day.

As we rolled into 2008, things started to change rapidly. The housing market collapsed, and the financial institutions melted down. We were all in uncharted territory. The effects were dramatic and immediate. Within four weeks, we had thirty-five trucks sitting in our parking lot. The builders stopped paying our invoices, and the financial imbalance ballooned to more than $600,000. Because of the lack of cash flow, the business died. As a personal guarantor for all the loans, I died financially with it. I was forced to file for bankruptcy.

The phone calls from those we owed money to tormented me. I was filled with shame, guilt, and confusion. I thought for sure God was going to heal my business. I was blessed to witness several miracles throughout my journey with Jesus, and I was convinced our business would be a testimony to His great power, but the business died, and I was devastated. I lost my beautiful home, SUV, and my childhood-dream sports car. At forty-four years old, I was forced to start over completely.

Much to my dismay, I was forced back into the field to work as a technician for another company. The only company that would pay me adequate money was sixty miles away, so I had a lot of drive time to contemplate and pray. I was angry, depressed, and confused.

I remember thinking, "God, I don't understand why this happened to me? I have been a faithful follower of you for many years—not only a tither but a generous giver, faithful in studying your Word and in prayer. I have tried to walk out the footsteps of Hosea, love my wife the way Jesus loved the church, and live as an *Image-Bearer* to my daughters. Why did this happen?"

> *Seek first the kingdom of God and His righteousness, and all these things shall be added to you.*
>
> *—Matthew 6:33*

Then I remember my soul being impressed with a message, not an audible voice, but a strong impression of Matthew 6:33: "Seek *first* the kingdom of God and His righteousness, and all these things shall be added to you" (emphasis mine). For the first time, I saw Matthew 6:33 as two distinct commands. *Seek first the kingdom of God* is the first command. The second command is to seek *His righteousness*, which is the command to salvation that we discussed in chapter 15, "The Perfect Wife." So, what does it mean to seek the kingdom of God? I believe it means to seek understanding and knowledge of the kingdom that the King has built. How was it designed to function? As I meditated on this, a memory from Amanda's childhood came back to me.

CHAPTER 20

N—NEVER FIGHT WITH GRAVITY

Amanda was two years old. She was in the backyard playing while I cleaned the pool. As I scooped leaves out of the deep end, I heard a loud bang on the kitchen window. Her mother was frantic and pointed to the pool. I looked down and saw Amanda at the bottom. Immediately, I dove in and rescued her from the water that enveloped her. Upon bringing her out, I realized she had instinctively held her breath.

"I went under," she said as she opened her eyes.

Upon reflection on this event, I began to wonder. What would have happened if I had not pulled Amanda out of the water? She would have drowned. Why would she have drowned? Very simply, because she was not designed to breathe water, and if she had died, it would not have made God mean, bad, or unjust. She would have died because gravity pulled her down under the water, and she is not designed to breathe under water. It is just a fact. It is the design of the kingdom.

Gravity is an interesting natural law. It is the invisible force that keeps all things grounded to the earth by the centrifugal motion of our planet spinning at an incredible rate of speed. Gravity allows us to stand upright and for cars to drive on roads. It is the silent pull that keeps us from floating and wandering to and fro in this world. We must respect this invisible force and honor it.

As humans, we have learned to respect gravity for what it is and recognize it as a force we cannot control. It just is, we believe it, and that settles it. I petition those things would function much better if we would honor the rest of the kingdom's design as much as we honor the law of gravity. We need to open our eyes, lift our heads, and look around us. Paul tells us in the book of Romans that God has made His invisible attributes by His visible creation. Therefore, we are without excuse. So, let's look at the *design*.

We are surrounded by designs or systems and natural laws: the solar system, respiratory system, and reproductive system, just to name a few. This is God's kingdom, and because He is the *Designer*, He is the King. There are also laws of nature, such as the law of electricity and the law of gravity.

These laws are meticulously designed. When honored, many of them can keep us alive, and when violated, they can take our lives. The *Design* does not change. The *Design* does not care what we think. The kingdom does not care if we like it or believe in it. Social status, ethnic groups, and age are nonfactors to the *Design*. They operate in the precise manner for which they are designed.

Upon further reflection of these concepts, I realized why my business failed. I had violated several laws of business. They are as precise and unchanging as the law of gravity. I violated principles regarding cash-flow management, purchasing through a PO system, and filing the appropriate liens. The business was destined to fail. Its failure was as inevitable as the destruction that follows a Category 4 hurricane slamming into the southwest coast of Florida.

The *Design* does not care *why* it is being violated. In my daughter's case, her death would have been sad and tragic because she did not know she was violating the design. However, in my case, I had no excuse. I knew better; the result was the same. The outcome was inevitable because the *Design* never changes. If there is a design, and as Christians, we believe there is, then God is the *Designer*.

In my opinion, there is no greater way to honor the *Designer* than honoring the *Design*. Conversely, there is no greater way to dishonor the *Designer* than to dishonor the *Design*. What is the original design of man? God formed man, Adam, and placed him in the garden of Eden. God instructed him to tend the garden and commanded him not to eat of the Tree of Knowledge of Good and Evil. Then God said, "It is not good for man to be alone," and made woman, as accounted for in Genesis 1. God's original design for man and woman was for them to rule and reign together as one. Partners and teammates.

You've heard the story many times about the serpent and Eve, which led to the fall of humanity. For many years, it bugged me that Adam got blamed, although technically, Eve was the one who ate first. The traditional teaching of this story states that Eve was deceived and Adam willfully disobeyed, creating what we commonly refer to as original sin.

> *There is no greater way to honor the* Designer *than honoring the* Design.

But I want to offer a different perspective. As we look closer at the passage, it is stated that Adam is *with* Eve when the dialogue with the serpent happens (Genesis 3:6). She then eats the fruit and hands it to Adam, her husband, who is *with* her. It is important to note here that God designed Adam first, brought him to life, and commanded him not to eat the fruit of that tree before Eve was ever created (Genesis 2:16). Therefore, Adam's designed responsibility was to communicate with Eve what God had said about the Tree of Knowledge of Good and Evil.

Adam should have intervened in the conversation between the serpent and Eve. He should have shut down the serpent and reminded Eve of God's goodness and the garden's beauty. This was all theirs to partake of and enjoy except for God's one command—to not eat from the Tree of Knowledge of Good and Evil. God also told Adam to be united with his wife. The two should become one.

Adam should have fought for them to remain united, not only with each other, but with God as well. He did not do that. He allowed her to disconnect not only from him and their union as husband and wife, but also from their unity with God. This is where Adam failed her as a husband. This is where he violated the *Original Design of Masculinity*. It is my perspective that this ultimately was the original sin of mankind: Adam violated the *Design* that God had for man.

The apostle Paul refers to Jesus as the Last Adam in 1 Corinthians 15:45. He makes the argument very plain. It's really a tale of two Adams. The first man, Adam, was shaped in God's image without a sinful nature and was designed by God to represent Him in the world as a man. Because of Adam's failure, Paul says that we are condemned to a life as a slave to sin and to an eternity in hell. But God already had a solution, and Jesus came to solve the problem. Born without a sinful nature and called to represent the Father in this fallen world, He lived a life without sin.

His sinless life would be offered as a sacrifice and save all who believed in Him and justify them by His blood. Jesus came as the Second Adam and restored, through His perfect obedience, the *Original Design* for man. He believed so deeply in God's design for mankind, that He was willing to fight to retain and restore it to the point of brutal crucifixion and death on a cross. Jesus walked out *God's Design for Masculinity*, not only as the Son of God but also as the Son of Man.

The last words Jesus spoke to us before He ascended to heaven are commonly referred to as "the Great Commission." Jesus commanded us to make disciples and teach them to obey all He has commanded. These words are so direct it is impossible to misinterpret them. This is the *Design* for the men who follow Jesus. We are designed *to be* disciples and *to make* disciples. What is a disciple, and how do we make disciples? This has been a topic of discussion for years as people have misinterpreted the words *believer* and *disciple* as synonyms. They are not. A believer is nothing more than a convert. I contend the spiritual condition of a man lies in one of four areas: unbeliever, convert, disciple, and Pharisee (religious zealot). Jesus designed us to be disciples.

The Word of God is very specific about defining the conditions of discipleship. Jesus said if we abide in His word, we are His disciple. He also told us if we love one another the way He loves us, we are His disciple. Jesus also said if we put no other relationship on earth ahead of our relationship with Him, we are His disciple. Jesus declared disciples would carry their cross and follow Him. If we knowingly and willingly violate God's Word, *God's Design*, we are not walking as a disciple.

Jesus laid out not only a specific criteria to live as a disciple but also a specific design to create disciples. This is commonly referred to as the fivefold ministry.

> And He Himself gave some to be apostles, some prophets, some evangelists, and some pastors and teachers, for the equipping of the saints for the work of ministry, for the edifying of the body of Christ, till we all come to the unity of the faith and of the knowledge of the Son of God, to a perfect man, to the measure of the stature of the fullness of Christ. (Ephesians 4:11–13)

This is Jesus's perfect *design* for making disciples.

In retrospect, my decision in 2012 to disconnect from the local church, discredit the majority of pastors, and attend church sporadically and on my terms is when my life went from bad to worse. I stopped being a disciple and became a convert. I have made many mistakes in my life. I believe this mistake is the most consequential because of the significant number of people and loved ones who suffered hurt and pain that I can directly link to this poor decision. Eight years of utter darkness. I had a plethora of reasons that included significant and unconscionable wounds. However, there is no excuse.

What does your church life look like? Are you a casual attender? Are you involved? Do you serve? Who is your pastor? It is impossible to claim to be a disciple of Jesus Christ and reject His *Design* of the local church. I understand this may be hard to read. It may cause anger and pain. I hate to admit it, but I ran around for years speaking against the church. I was doing my own Bible studies, leading others to Jesus, and praying with people in their homes. I had swallowed the lie I was able to function outside of *God's Design*.

This may require work on your part. You may have to visit several churches before finding one that holds to the supremacy of God's Word, has robust worship, and has dynamic ministries for your family. It may require that you drive a significant distance to attend such a church. I want to caution you. This journey will take time.

As you go down this road, your encouragement is found in Genesis 8:22:

> While the earth remains,
> Seedtime and harvest,
> Cold and heat,
> Winter and summer,
> And day and night
> Shall not cease.

In this world, there is a specific order for creation. I like to think of it as three separate events, which involve seed, time, and harvest. It makes sense if you think about it. This *God-Designed* order applies to all areas of life: plants, trees, animals, and humans. It even applies to the cause and effect of the decisions we make.

Consider the system of reproduction for a moment. When a husband and wife decide they are ready to start a family, a certain course of events must take place for the child's conception. First, the husband must plant the seed into the wife. Through the fertilization process, conception takes place. Then it's implanted inside the woman's womb. In order for the baby to viably enter the world, a period of time must pass for the child to develop and grow in the mother's womb. Finally, when the time has passed, the baby is born, and they celebrate the birth. "For You formed my inward parts; You covered me in my mother's womb" (Psalm 139:13). Seed, time, and harvest is a natural process and another part of *God's Design* for this world.

The changes you are about to make on your journey are equivalent to planting new seed. All seeds have a gestational period. Your job is to water the seed and keep it healthy. Keep reading your Bible, partner with other believers, and get connected to your local church. Eventually, the harvest will come.

Also, be prepared. Before the harvest of all the good seeds comes to fruition, we must endure the harvest of the bad seed we planted prior to our decision to change our journey and walk with the Lord. So, don't get discouraged when the bad harvest comes. Keep pressing on. Trust the new seed you have planted. I believe this is what Paul was referring to when he said, "Let us not grow weary while doing good [planting good seed], for in due season [time] we shall reap [harvest] if we do not lose heart" (Galatians 6:9).

Now I read Matthew 6:33 differently. Seek first the *Design*, honor the *Designer by honoring* the *Design*, and all of these things will be added to me. It leads me to contemplate what law of gravity, or what *Design(s) of God*, I am violating in my life.

I challenge you to look at every area of your life through the prism of design. Think

> *Seek first the* Design, *honor the* Designer by honoring *the* Design, *and all of these things will be added to me.*

about your relationships. How about your physical fitness and wellness? What about the design for education and personal growth? Consider the design for every aspect of life. Everything. I encourage you to be proactive in your venture. Don't wait for the problem to manifest. When I waited to address the design of my mental health, it almost cost me my life.

I encourage you not to leave any stone unturned as you seek to pursue God's kingdom and *His Design* for your life. It is Jesus's will that we have life and that we have it more abundantly. For us to enjoy His blessing, we must enter into rest through faith and belief in God's perfect *Design: His Design for Masculinity*.

O—OWN YOUR DECISIONS

September 11, 2001, changed the world. I remember that morning well. I was working in a home installing cable television. My heart immediately went to the passengers, flight attendants, and pilots. As time passed and weeks rolled by, I saw a connection between our everyday lives and what happened on 9/11/01. We are all called to be the pilot of our own plane, our life journey. We are responsible as men not only to fly our lives safely and correctly but to take our families along as passengers.

My entire life, I have fought being extremely impulsive, driven by my senses. Emotions, feelings, and senses are all a gift from God. Their design is to assist me through life and to give me feedback about myself. While thinking about the tragedy on 9/11/01, I saw my senses from a whole different perspective. I view our emotions, feelings, and senses very similarly to flight attendants.

The role of a flight attendant is essential in air travel. They help make the journey safe and comfortable, but flight attendants were not designed to fly the plane. If a flight attendant were to go into the cockpit, seize control of the plane, and start flying it, we would call them a terrorist. When a terrorist seizes control, only devastation and destruction follow. Similarly, when my emotions, feelings, and impulses seize control of the trajectory of my life and the decisions I make, then surely, destruction and devastation will follow.

Here are some questions we have to ask ourselves:

- What are we allowing entry into the cockpit of our plane?
- Have we invited fear, anger, lust, or unforgiveness?
- Are fits of rage, bitterness, jealousy, rejection, or greed flying the plane? Have we become their slaves because of our obedience to them?
- Do we feed them and provide them with an environment to thrive?

These feelings, emotions, and triggers are real. Most of them are part of *God's Original Design* for humanity. They were gifts given to us to assist us along our journey through life. They were never intended to have control of our lives. When they are fed, nurtured, and surrendered to, they hold us captive, much like those terrorists did on that fateful day in September 2001.

My terrorists were "regret" and "worry." As humans created in the image of God, we are not designed to carry these emotions. Regret has to do with my past, and worry pertains to future things to come. The cross of Christ dealt with both. Jesus saved us from our past, present, and future sins.

Paul said in Philippians 4:8, "Finally, brethren, whatever things are true, whatever things are noble, whatever things are just, whatever things are pure, whatever things are lovely, and whatever things are of good report, if there is any virtue and if there is anything praiseworthy—meditate on these things." He also said in Philippians 3:13, "Forgetting those things which are behind and reaching forward to those things which are ahead." Therefore, I must let go of worry and release regret. My body was not designed to carry them.

For over two decades, every night as I lay in bed, I fed the terrorists of my mind with toxic thoughts and negative inputs from all directions. Dwelling on these things fueled the terrorists even more, and I became unhealthy. I had virtually fallen into an emotional swimming pool in which I was not designed to breathe. Regret and worry had enveloped me, suffocating peace and joy out of my lungs. I was no longer flying the plane. I had become a helpless passenger.

The most skilled pilots are the ones you want flying your plane through inclement weather and horrible storms. They have the designation of being instrument-rated pilots. They are trained to use their instrument panels and trust the information from those sources more than *what* they may see or feel as they fly. That is our ultimate goal: free to be the pilot, not the passenger.

We are set free, so we can trust the instrument panel for our lives, which is God's Word. We need to fly as the pilot of our plane, relying on the instrument panels God gave us— guidance from the Holy Spirit, the Bible, and fellowship with other believers.

Talking with men about these issues, I have discovered that this is the desire of most of their hearts. We genuinely want to walk the walk, not just talk the talk. Let's reflect on this. Where is the disconnection between leading our families according to *God's Design* for manhood, and being driven by our senses, emotions, and feelings? We are surrounded by emotional rants on social media, road rage on our highways, and men just retreating into isolation.

I know what it is like to feel powerless to change. Sometimes, we just feel trapped on the roller coaster of life, being pulled to and fro, having no idea where we are going or what lies around the next corner. At this point, we give ourselves the pep talk, "Things will be different next time, and I'm going to do better," only to find ourselves back in the same place again. For me, it was because of the deep wounds I had never addressed. I assumed I could just manage my pain, but I was wrong.

Beware of Painkillers

We are all aware of painkillers. In the literal sense, this is in no way a judgement or indictment on anyone who takes painkillers. I've had four major surgeries and several serious sports injuries, so I understand there are times when we need pain medication. What is interesting about pain medication is there are usually two warnings on the bottle. One is, "Do not operate heavy machinery," and the other warning states, "May cause drowsiness."

Another negative side effect of pain medication is your body builds up a tolerance to it. As a result, the longer you take it, the more you will need for it to be effective at numbing the pain. Typically, as people increase their dosage, they become more dependent on the pain medication, making them more private about their attempts to numb their pain. What pain medication are you taking? Have you increased the dosage? Are you drowsy?

I'll never forget the day I realized I had fallen asleep. Bear in mind, I wasn't sleeping but asleep nonetheless. I was working more than sixty hours a week and was incredibly involved with my children's lives and more, but had fallen asleep spiritually because my pain medication caused drowsiness. My wounds were real, and the majority of them were inflicted by others. The reality was that I had resorted to various types of medication to numb my pain.

Take a moment and look at yourself. Truly dig down deep and be honest about your current status of manhood.

- Do you hurt?
- What wounds do you have?
- What disappointments, disillusionments, or failures are gnawing at your heart?
- What is your pain medicine of choice?
- Is it drugs, alcohol, pornography, or sex outside of *God's Design*?
- Have you turned to money, success, approval, physical appearance, or social media to numb the pain?

It doesn't really matter what the pain medicine is because they all cause drowsiness.

Continuing in the spirit of transparency, I had been numbing myself for so long that I simply fell asleep. Paul says in Ephesians 5:14:

> Awake, you who sleep,
> Arise from the dead,
> And Christ will give you light.

Wake up, men! It is time to put down the pain medication. We must walk in the *light*.

Paul talks about walking in darkness and keeping things in secret when writing 1 Corinthians 4:2. We used to live in darkness prior to knowing Jesus, but now we walk in the light. The hidden places have been revealed so we can make the necessary changes and press on towards the goal.

John 3:16–19 addresses this very topic and states that men hated the light and hid in the darkness because they were afraid their deeds would be exposed. It is impossible for us to find healing in the darkness. James echoes this point when he states that we are to confess our sins one to another so that we may be healed. When we confess our sins to God, we are forgiven, and when we confess our sins to one another, we are healed. This takes us back to the *Original Design*.

Adam was designed to be naked and unashamed, which means fully transparent and honest before God and man. After he fell, he clothed himself to hide from mankind and God. Jesus, our Redeemer, later came as the Second Adam and restored the *Design* of being fully transparent and living in the light. While walking on this earth, Jesus had different levels of relationships. Even though Jesus had many followers, some were closer to Him than others. He had the 72, the 12, and then the 3—James, Peter, and John.

Different levels of relationship do not mean preferential treatment. Remember, Jesus treated Judas with the same love He treated the rest of the disciples. James, Peter, and John experienced a level of transparency with Jesus that the others did not. They went with Him to the Mount of Transfiguration and stayed nearby while He prayed in the garden of Gethsemane.

It is key we walk in wisdom as we pursue this life of transformation, living naked and unashamed. We must surround ourselves with a few like-minded men. Men who love Jesus and His Word. This gives us a place of complete and safe transparency. Transparency with purpose keeps us in the light. The enemy cannot operate in the light. As we shine the light on the dark places inside, we will remain in Jesus.

We can then be the pilot of our own plane, with the Holy Spirit as our GPS, guiding and illuminating our path. Our decisions will be Spirit-led instead of being led by the flesh or the enemy. They will be principle-based, not driven by impulse or reaction. By doing so, we will make it to our desired destination.

> *Transparency with purpose keeps us in the light.*

Beware of Being Tired and Hungry

The story of Esau is easily overlooked. I feel Esau is one of the most important biblical characters to be studied. He was the first-born son of Isaac. Abraham was his grandfather, and the blessing of Abraham, along with all it entailed, was rightfully his. The Bible states Esau returned from the field after he was out hunting. He was tired and hungry. It sounds a lot like us. His younger brother, also his twin, Jacob, had made some stew.

Esau asked Jacob for some, and Jacob responded by telling Esau to give him his birthright in return for food. Esau questioned what the value of his birthright would be if he died. In other words, "I really don't care about my birthright. Food and rest are more important to me." Through a very simple business transaction, Jacob took the blessing and lineage of Israel through his family in exchange for his stew.

Much has been said about this passage, primarily focusing on the deceitfulness of Jacob. In fact, the Hebrew name for Jacob means *Deceiver*. Jacob later wrestled with God, who then changed his name to Israel. So, the character of Esau seems relatively inconsequential. However, in the book of Hebrews, the writer brings him to the forefront. He called Esau a "fornicator or profane person . . . , [who] for one morsel of food sold his birthright. For you know that afterward, when he wanted to inherit the blessing, he was rejected, because he found no place for repentance, though he sought it diligently with tears" (Hebrews 12:16–17).

This gives us a fuller picture of what happened. Esau caused his own demise. The inheritance and the blessing were rightfully his. He wanted the blessing so much that he sought it diligently through tears. This is how regret looks.

According to the verse, the fact he sought the blessing meant it was a continual pursuit. He had a perpetual ache for the blessing, yet he was rejected. Why? Because he refused to repent. His uncontrolled appetites became his driving force. Hebrews 12:16 calls him a "fornicator or profane person," which is a condition of the heart, not simply a one-time event. The truth is, Esau gave up his blessing for the momentary pleasure of feeding his body.

Esau wanted to feed both his appetite and the blessing simultaneously. The Bible is clear that you cannot eat from both the Tree of Knowledge of Good and Evil *and* the Tree of Life. Furthermore, you cannot sit at both tables—the Table of the Lord *and* the Table of Satan. You cannot serve two masters. God *and* money. Fresh water and bitter water cannot come from the same well, and you cannot walk in the flesh *and* walk in the Spirit at the same time. There is a choice, and we must choose one or the other.

The challenge with the story of Esau is that he allowed his God-given appetite for food to get out of control. Paul tells us we must be aware of the schemes and strategies of the enemy. I believe one of his greatest tactics is taking God-given gifts and letting them get out of control. We all have natural appetites. The appetite for food. The appetite for sex. The appetite for approval from people. The appetite for money, and the list goes on. However, they must always remain within God's design and under the Holy Spirit's control. If not, they will morph into something that will consume and destroy our lives.

Our birthright, our family lineage as a child of God, must always be a dominant force in our lives. I know this is not easy, and it requires us to surrender our lives, thoughts, and actions to the sovereignty of God. God is with us and will honor our submission to his authority over our lives. Another important takeaway is that God cannot and will not be manipulated by our tears, emotions, or excuses.

Looking back at my own life, I am astonished how good I was at lying to myself. I was Esau. Crying, broken, and sad.

> *Repentance is the proof of desire.*

I told myself I wanted the things of God, and I would wait on Him to move in my life. All the while, I continued to feed my appetites. The truth is, I did not truly desire the things of God enough to submit to his lordship. Neither did Esau. *Repentance is the proof of desire.*

People will go to great lengths and do almost anything to get what they desire. If there is not a pursuit, or a lack of willingness to change, repent, or surrender, then there is no desire. The promise in God's Word is those who *diligently seek Him* will be rewarded.

So where are you? How are your appetites doing? Have you gotten so numb that you stopped crying or caring? If so, I encourage you to find someone to talk to, because it is a very dangerous place. The warning to Cain was, "Sin is crouching at your door; it desires to have you, but you must rule over it" (Genesis 4:7 NIV).

Uncontrolled appetites and painkillers will enslave your soul. That is exactly what the enemy desires for you because he has come to steal, kill, and destroy. But Jesus has come to set the captives free. It is *God's Design* that, as men, we walk in freedom. This is our call to manhood.

CHAPTER 22

W—WIN THE DAY

In 2005, the housing market was on fire. As a result, my company grew rapidly. In an attempt to be the best leader possible, I was always on the lookout for excellent leadership books. I recognized leadership and godly manhood were intricately linked. God designed men to be leaders. Whether we function in the role of husband, father, coworker, or church member, the mantle of leadership rests upon our shoulders. Throughout this journey together, I have recommended several books that have profoundly impacted me. Another book that significantly influenced and altered my thought process for the rest of my life was *The Carolina Way* by Dean Smith.

The Dean Smith Story

Dean Smith was the head basketball coach at the University of North Carolina. Arguably, he was one of the greatest basketball coaches of all time. He won 75 percent of the games he coached over thirty-six years, and his most notable player was

Michael Jordan. While I was reading his book, there was one small comment he made that both shocked and challenged me. He said he never looked at the scoreboard during the game.

Smith went on to say he simply focused on each individual possession to ensure his team executed the principles of basketball that he believed produced winning games. If they submitted to the principles of winning basketball, the scoreboard would take care of itself.

I sat back in my chair and thought about it. I was amazed. As a society, we have become scoreboard watchers. We elevate its significance because the scoreboard determines who wins, right? As I thought about it, the scoreboard doesn't really determine who wins. It is simply a report or a by-product of what is happening in the game.

The more I contemplated that, the more it made sense. If the scoreboard was the end all, be all, how you played the game would be irrelevant. The only thing that mattered was winning. The end would justify the means. Yet intrinsically, we all know that statement not to be true.

Coach Smith believed if you played the game according to the *principles* that produced winning, instead of focusing on the points, the team would win on a higher level of consistency. It is possible to have a sloppy win occasionally. Despite the win, you must correct the disciplines that were violated. Not making changes and celebrating the victory is playing with fire. Samson is an excellent example of someone who celebrated his wins while ignoring the disciplines. Don't play the game of life like Samson. Play it like Michael Jordan.

Michael Jordan was a protégé and disciple of Dean Smith. Jordan played basketball as if the score was 0-0. Every possession throughout every game, in his mind, the score was still

0-0. He sold out to the processes of basketball and was not enamored with the outcome. Both Jordan and Smith recognized that if you focus on the process that produces winning, the results will become a natural by-product.

We could list several other stories of people who have achieved great things, whether it be Tiger Woods, one of the greatest golfers of all time, or Nolan Ryan, who threw the most no-hitters in baseball history. Yet, the story is always the same. Stay in the moment. Focus on the *now*. Even Jesus said, "So don't worry about tomorrow, for tomorrow will bring its own worries. Today's trouble is enough for today" (Matthew 6:34 NLT).

As you embark on the journey to return to the *Original Design for Masculinity* for which you were created to walk, please do not make a long list of things you will never do again or have some scoreboard that accounts for everything you did right. Throw away the scoreboard. Live every day as 0-0.

It will be a journey you walk one day at a time. Focus on being faithful with where you are, what you say, and what you do for today. Remember, the score is 0-0 until you reach the end of the game and meet your Savior in heaven. Then you will hear Him say to you, "Well done, good and faithful servant" (Matthew 25:21).

Control the Controllables

So, how do I win the day? Control the controllables. I am in control of what time I go to bed and wake up. I control what I eat emotionally, physically, and mentally. Therefore, I am responsible for making choices and decisions that produce the abundant, powerful, and impactful life I am designed to have. We are called to be overcomers.

Accept the fact you cannot do this alone. Jesus sent the disciples out two-by-two for a reason. You will need other men to walk with you. Be aware as you go down this road that sometimes your life's outward appearance will not change. In fact, it might even get worse. Just remember seed, time, and harvest. Keep planting good seeds. In due time, you will reap the rewards of your harvest, but first, you will have to endure the harvest of the bad seeds.

I'll never forget one day I was in the gym talking to a group of guys, sharing some of the things in this book. One of the guys said, "Jim, why should we listen to you? Your life is a wreck!"

At the time, I was recently divorced after twenty-eight years of marriage. I was running a new business, which was an evident struggle. I no longer owned a home, and my work truck was my personal car. Definitely not where I thought I would be in my fifties.

"Because it's about serving the kingdom," I said. "It's not a success system. Jesus is not Tony Robbins. In fact, if you look at His life, quite often, it looked like He was failing. They mocked Him while He hung on the cross." We have to let the external results go and trust the design. *God's Design*.

It's about doing our best daily, surrendering to God's will, submitting to His Word, and loving others the way Jesus loves us. The days we do that well, we can lay our head down at night and thank the Lord for giving us the strength to get through another twenty-four hours. On the days we don't do it well, we must lay it at the foot of the cross, make ourselves accountable to somebody, let it go, then live to fight one more day.

The truth is, life is hard. This is going to be a difficult journey. Quite often, it may cause you to suffer. Paul says, "I want to know Christ and experience the mighty power that raised him from the dead. I want to suffer with him, sharing in his death" (Philippians 3:10 NLT).

A Living Sacrifice

Peter reminds us we are called to suffer. I am not, in any way, trying to be negative or take the wind out of your sails. But this is a call to walk in the life of a disciple for which we are designed. Suffering is part of the design. Jesus tells us we have to count the cost. The life of a disciple is one of self-sacrifice and following in Jesus's footsteps. Jesus said He "did not come to be served, but to serve, and to give his life as a ransom for many" (Mark 10:45 NIV).

You can only accomplish this lifestyle one day at a time. God sent His angels to minister to Jesus in the garden of Gethsemane. In the same way, He will minister to you. I encourage you to keep your eyes open and look for Him in the mundane, daily grind of life. At

> *The life of a disciple is one of self-sacrifice and following in Jesus's footsteps.*

some unexpected moment, He will show Himself to encourage you. He will breathe on you and put wind underneath your wings. So be on the lookout.

One night, I was running a service call shortly after we started our new air conditioning company in 2013. I was working seven days a week, twelve to fourteen hours a day. I was exhausted, bitter from the wounds of my past, and quite frankly, not in a good place. On my way home, my daughter called to tell me another service call had come in. It was dark, I was tired, and I just wanted to go home. However, I couldn't, because the property manager we worked for required me to run this call.

When I arrived, I rang the doorbell, and as the door opened, I was greeted by the smiling face of a little boy named Josiah. He was so excited I had come to fix his air conditioner. My heart melted. Despite no longer being in the youth ministry, I never lost my love for being around kids.

"Hey, Josiah, do you want to be my helper while I work on your air conditioner?"

"Yes!" he eagerly said with a smile.

For the next thirty to forty-five minutes, he was my sidekick. As I finished the job and spoke with his mother, he whispered in her ear. She started to chuckle.

She said, "I'll ask Mr. Jim," and turned to me. "Josiah wants to know if you will take communion with him." He had the elements in his hand. They had kept the individual communion cups with the wafer and juice.

"Yes, I'd love to share communion with you!"

I was completely overwhelmed. I knelt, prayed over the elements, and shared communion with a little boy who melted my heart and brought me to my knees. I cried all the way home. It was evident God was speaking to me, despite my scoreboard looking terrible. Although I was losing in life and even losing spiritually, God was still working. He showed me I was not alone, and He was with me.

After that moment, I became more mindful of looking for the handprints of God in my daily life. I challenge you to do this as well. He's leading you on a journey. His plans for you are bigger than your plans. He sees things you cannot see. He can orchestrate events for your good, even though they look like they are going to harm you. You can't quit. You just have to refuse to quit, my friend.

There's an amazing song by Mercy Me called "Even If." I sang this song repeatedly during this season of my life. It is based on the story of Shadrach, Meshach, and Abednego when they told King Nebuchadnezzar their God could save them, but even if He did not, they refused to bow down to the king's idol (Daniel 3:17–18). Arm yourself with their attitude as you fight this daily battle because it's not about this life. We've been bought at a price, and our lives are not our own.

Redemption Wins

Trust God's Word and His promises. One of His promises is that He will restore what the locusts have eaten (Joel 2:25), and He did that in my life. The year 2020 was a very difficult year for many people, in which the locusts ran wild. COVID-19 paralyzed the world. The year 2020 was also a painfully difficult year for Mindy and me, although we had not yet met at this point.

Both of us had spent the past twenty-five-plus years serving God the best we knew how in our respective lives. We both found ourselves divorced and surrounded by pain and trauma. The economy was unstable, and I was afraid of another failed business. This triggered all of my old feelings of inadequacy and sent me into a downward spiral. It was reminiscent of my years of being a victim, and I was tempted to turn to painkillers.

That summer, Mindy felt God's call upon her life to move to Florida in the middle of the pandemic. It didn't make sense, but she followed His lead. Just prior to her move, her father passed away. Her mother had open heart surgery and died six weeks after her father. She was living in a new state, with a new job teaching during COVID-19, along with the numerous challenges the educational system faced.

We were both stretched to our limits by the time autumn rolled around, and it didn't seem like there was any end in sight. I had finally returned to daily prayer and devotions. I found a new church and was getting involved again after a long hiatus. Mindy tried to connect to a church in her new community, too, although many churches still hadn't fully opened back up. It was a challenging time for us both, to say the least.

We met in December and immediately felt spiritually rejuvenated. Despite our being battered, broken, and looking defeated externally, we began the journey together. When we met, we left no topic untouched. We were vulnerable, transparent, and completely honest with our past, wounds, and triggers. As part of the dating process, she and I read daily devotions and prayed together. We sought God with everything in us, and He filled us with peace.

In June of 2021, I recall being aware of the feeling that I no longer hurt inside. I realized memories that would have triggered pain several months earlier now produced gratitude. Interestingly enough, the memories were still there, and I could still see the horrific events in my mind's eye, but I had become grateful for my relationship with Mindy. Upon further reflection, I had the epiphany I would not have been as grateful had I not had the pain of my past. I remembered thinking, *Wow! Truly all things work together for good, to those who love God and are called according to His purpose* (Romans 8:28).

By this time, I knew Mindy's birthday was approaching. She had mentioned it was in August, but I didn't really put much thought into it. As August rolled around, I recognized her birthday was the twenty-eighth. August 28 *is* 8:28. Again, I was overwhelmed by the goodness of God as I realized *Mindy is my 8:28*. He took all my trials, traumas, and temptations and worked them together for my good. The Bible says God shows partiality to no man, which means what He has done for me, He will do for you, and freedom starts N.O.W. So, win the day, my friend.

WIN the day!

If you enjoyed this book, will you consider sharing the message with others?

Let us know your thoughts. You can let the author know by visiting or sharing a photo of the cover on our social media pages or leaving a review at a retailer's site. All of it helps us get the message out!

Email: info@ironstreammedia.com

 @ironstreammedia

---

Iron Stream, Iron Stream Fiction, Iron Stream Kids, Brookstone Publishing Group, and Life Bible Study are imprints of Iron Stream Media, which derives its name from Proverbs 27:17, "As iron sharpens iron, so one person sharpens another." This sharpening describes the process of discipleship, one to another. With this in mind, Iron Stream Media provides a variety of solutions for churches, ministry leaders, and nonprofits ranging from in-depth Bible study curriculum and Christian book publishing to custom publishing and consultative services.

For more information on ISM and its imprints, please visit IronStreamMedia.com